LESSONS LEARNED ON THE WAY DOWN

"Bernie Brown knows what it means to Lead Like Jesus. Telling stories from his 30+ year career as a distinguished health care executive and educator, Bernie shows how he put Christian leadership to work in the secular world. These highly readable recollections will touch your heart and help you bridge the gap between your career path and your faith journey."
—**Ken Blanchard,** Coauthor of *The One Minute Manager* © and Cofounder of **Lead Like Jesus**

"Bernie Brown's **Lessons Learned on the Way Down** made me laugh and remember. I laughed because I was there for some of the same events. I remembered because I was often a recipient of his teachings as I watched him put his faith in action. Bernie has always been a keen observer of the lessons of life."
—**Honorable Roy Barnes,** Governor, State of Georgia 1999-2003

"**Lessons Learned on the Way Down** is intriguing and inspiring. Its very practical nature is illustrated from Bernie Brown's own life and experience. I would enthusiastically recommend its use."
—**Bishop Richard Looney,** Foundation for Evangelism, United Methodist Church

"As I read the stories in **Lessons Learned on the Way Down,** I found myself identifying, laughing and agreeing with the life lessons shared by Bernie Brown. In a humble way, he has shown why servant leadership results in a fulfilling, rewarding and joyous life. The stories are great examples of a leader trying with God's help to lead like the greatest leader of all times – Jesus."
—**James "Micky" Blackwell,** Executive Vice President, Lockheed Martin Corporation (Ret.)

"**Lessons Learned on the Way Down** can help you live up to your leadership potential. These lessons come from the refining fires of the long and productive career of one who practiced what he herein professes. Reading it will prove to be an exercise in personal development."

—**Dr. Nelson Price,** Pastor Emeritus, Roswell Street Baptist Church (National Board Chairman, Fellowship of Christian Athletes 1999-2005)

"I have always considered Bernie Brown to be a real pro. In **Lessons Learned on the Way Down**, he shares insights gained in a career of seeking to lead the Christian way."

—**Neely Young,** Editor-in-Chief, *Georgia Trend Magazine*

"As a nurse, I know what it means to be on the frontline of service in a hospital. It was obvious to me when visiting Bernie Brown's organization that he truly sought to empower his frontline employees by 'leading from the bottom.' That principle is the basis of **Lessons Learned on the Way Down**."

—**Kaye Lani Rafko-Wilson,** Miss America 1988

"Throughout his brilliant career, Bernie has been a diligent student even as he was leading and teaching others. **Lessons Learned on the Way Down** offers insight, a lot of soul searching, plenty of encouragement, and personal growth for those who will spend a bit of time pondering its offerings."

—**Larry Sanders,** CEO, Columbus Regional Health System (Chairman, Board of Governors, American College of Healthcare Executives 2003-04)

LESSONS
LEARNED ON
THE WAY
DOWN

A Perspective
On Christian Leadership
In a Secular World
(Including a guide for individual or group study)

Bernie Brown

Bernie Brown

Inspiring Voices books may be ordered through booksellers or by contacting:

Inspiring Voices
1663 Liberty Drive
Bloomington, IN 47403
www.inspiringvoices.com
1-(866) 697-5313

ISBN: 978-1-4624-0350-9 (sc)
ISBN: 978-1-4624-0351-6 (e)

Library of Congress Control Number: 2012917909

Printed in the United States of America

Inspiring Voices rev. date: 10/02/2012

DEDICATION

To all my families from whom I learned:
My immediate and extended one;
My organizational ones;
My church one; and
My universal one,
The family of
GOD

ACKNOWLEDGMENTS

Some of the ideas presented in this book originated with others. Where known, credit was given. However, because some are unknown, I would like this to be an acknowledgment of appreciation to all whose words and ideas were of help to me in learning the lessons contained herein.

Additionally, as always my wife, Snookie, contributed greatly as my editor-for-life, and my former executive assistant, Doris Reidy provided assistance over the years and graciously authored the foreword to this book. Others have supported this effort in various encouraging ways, some even to the point of endorsing and recommending it. I have included a special tribute to Nathan (see Epilogue).

The preparation of this work, while somewhat demanding and tedious because I am not a seasoned writer, has been a labor of love and a real blessing. It has kept me busy and out of my wife's way in her castle, our home. However, more importantly it has allowed me the opportunity to revisit some of my past career experiences and be reminded how good God is.

To God be the Glory.

Contents

WHY A THIRD EDITION?
"Bridging the Gap"

After writing a story the author will often look back and wish that another thought could have been conveyed or perhaps an additional chapter included. A second edition of a work can provide just such an opportunity, assuming, of course, that the first edition is sufficiently well received in order to justify a second. But a third edition...why?

The first two editions of *Lessons Learned on the Way Down* have primarily been sold and used in my home region (Atlanta, Georgia and North Carolina). The third edition will be marketed nationally through *Inspiring Voices*, the publishing service of *Guideposts*. This book is being re-published concurrent with the release of my new one entitled *Purpose in the Fourth Quarter, Finishing the Game of Life Victoriously*, also by *Inspiring Voices*. The proceeds from the sale of both books will benefit several church, community, and educational organizations.

I was deeply honored when Ken Blanchard, coauthor of *The One Minute Manager*, agreed to endorse my book. Interestingly, he commented, "These highly readable recollections will...help you bridge the gap between your career path and your faith journey." That description really struck a chord with me as well as many who have read the book.

As a result, I became involved in a Christian leadership conference series entitled "Bridging the Gap between Your Career Path and Faith Journey." The inaugural program was held in the spring of 2009 at Epworth by the Sea, St. Simon's Island, GA (United Methodist Conference and Retreat Center). At that conference, we explored how we can more effectively apply Christian principles in the sports arena, in educational institutions, in the business world, in music and in the "limelight." The role of the church itself in bridging the gap was given special emphasis. Since then several other local and regional conferences, retreats and workshops have been held in other venues.

There are two main additions included since the first edition. The first is another chapter (Chapter 10) entitled "A Lesson That Should have been Learned at Church," challenging churches to champion Christian leadership development. The second is an update on our grandson, Nathan's battle with cancer and our family's continuing spiritual journey. My wife, Snookie, and I share this with you from the grandparents' perspective in the Epilogue.

"Bernie's little book project," as Snookie calls it, has been a fascinating experience for this modest scribe. I started over 40 years ago with a monthly newsletter column and ended with a book that shares many of the ensuing lessons learned on the way down. During this journey, I remember stopping at every juncture along the way and praying, "Heavenly Father, may this humble effort bring honor to you!" And that is still my prayer. Maybe that's the key!!

In addition to learning our lessons on the way down, I sincerely hope that we all will bridge the gap between our career paths and faith journeys.

"BRIDGING THE GAP"

There is a gap 'tween God and me;
Must bridge that gap so I can be
Someone who finds that long lost key.
Please God come down and set me free.

I live a life that's all 'bout me;
The world says take and I agree.
Fortune and fame are what I seek,
Yet peace and joy I cannot keep.

The Word came down, said "follow me;"
I did just that, now I can see.
He gave his life on a rugged tree.
I met Him there at Calvary.

We bridged that gap 'tween God and me;
And praise to Him I now can be
One who has found that long lost key.
He rose again and set me free!

I hope you enjoy the Third Edition.

Bernie Brown
2012

FOREWORD

During the sixteen years that I worked as Bernie Brown's executive assistant, I had a ringside seat to watch his leadership theories in action. It was a post-graduate course in leading people and convinced me that *relationships* are at the heart of every job. The smartest person in the room will fail without the cooperation of others.

Bernie is a Christian and his beliefs influence every aspect of his life. If he never said a word about his faith, you could discern it from his actions. He is genuinely interested in all the folks he meets—their families, their work, what they do for fun, books they've read lately, what is worrying them or making them happy—and they open up in the warmth of his attention. I think that quality, more than any other, is what made him a successful CEO. Lots of people have an MBA; Bernie also has an MPA: Master of Personal Affirmation.

How did these qualities translate into his leadership style? Here's an example. First thing every day he made his rounds, greeting everyone with an enthusiastic, "Good Morning! How are you today?" There was only one acceptable response: "Great!" We learned that being fine or o.k. didn't cut it. We had to be GREAT and we had to say it like we meant it. And somehow, despite some grumbling, we found we did mean it. It set the tone for the day.

Bernie sang on the job. He whistled, told corny jokes, clapped his hands loudly to wake us up and made life a little lighter as he conducted the serious business of running hospitals. On days when there wasn't a noon meeting, he brought his lunch in a "Brown bag" and ate with the staff in the break room, a time noted for outbreaks of hilarity. He took some unmerciful kidding and laughed hardest when the joke was on him.

Of course, there were challenging times, days filled with difficult decisions, deadlines and disappointments. I sometimes saw him get mad, but I never saw him get even. His credo, voiced in a variety of situations, was, "Do what's right. All things work together for good..." Under Bernie's leadership, we never lost sight of our mission.

Whether it was one's job to perform surgery, attend at the bedside, fold linens or type memos, we were all part of a team caring for patients with passion and dedication.

He says he was always learning from others, but he was always teaching, too, often in the form of parables. In the stories that follow, you'll read in his own words the lessons he learned and taught, exemplifying his spirit of servant leadership.

You'll see that *LESSONS LEARNED ON THE WAY DOWN* are keepers.

Doris Reidy
(The Author's Executive Assistant for 16 years until his retirement)

PREFACE

To rise to the position of "leader" in an organization, institution or any team is viewed as the ultimate accomplishment. The title of chief of something (i.e., CEO, president, director, superintendent, bishop, senior minister, captain, admiral, general, head coach, etc.) carries with it great status and reward. Because of this, most aspiring leaders spend their lives attempting to climb their organizational ladders to reach the highest possible perch. To advance, corporate workers aspire to be supervisors, supervisors aspire to be managers, managers aspire to be vice-presidents and vice presidents aspire to be the president. Then what? When they have arrived at their ultimate perches, what then? Can they handle their roles as leaders? Is it what they thought it would be? Will those to be led follow the leader?

Unfortunately, "leadership" is losing its luster in our society today. With the indictment and conviction of corporate executives, corruption among top government officials, misconduct by religious leaders, and the like constantly in the news, the leader perch is becoming more precarious. Yet, is not the need for authentic, effective leadership more evident than ever in our organizations and institutions?

I feel somewhat qualified to respond to these and many other relative questions, because I have been there. I may even be uniquely qualified because I reached my professional pinnacle at a relatively young age. I became the Administrator of a major hospital at the age of 31 with no previous chief executive experience and spent the next 30 years learning how to be its leader. When appointed, my institution's annual budget was $10 million and it employed around 700. When I retired thirty years later as CEO, the health care system which had evolved had a budget of $1.5 billion with a workforce of almost 18,000. What an adventure! How did it work? What worked? What did not?

During those 30 years, I wrote and recorded many of my experiences in numerous professional journals and periodicals, three books and more than 300 newsletter columns. I spoke at local, regional and national functions, consulted and led numerous workshops, retreats and conferences, and taught leadership courses at the graduate school level at a major university.

Throughout my career, I searched constantly for lessons that I could apply and share in the area of leadership. For example, during one entire year I focused on a fascinating book which contained everything I needed to know about my work, my role and even my life in an organizational setting. I have continued to use it and reference it constantly because as a result of that year of study, my job became my ministry. I would highly recommend it to any current or aspiring leader. It can be purchased at any book store and is entitled *THE HOLY BIBLE.*

Even though my entire professional career was spent in private and government settings which were all secular in nature, I learned that Christian leadership principles could still be applied there. In fact, it was exciting to have a ministry in the real world of business and human services. In my opinion, it also makes *good business sense* to lead an organization God's way.

The purpose of this literary effort, which I call *LESSONS LEARNED ON THE WAY DOWN,* is to share some of my findings from a career of research and practice in the field of *leadership* from a Christian perspective. It would be impossible to address all the issues one might face as a leader of a team or organization. Therefore, I have chosen a representative sample of the lessons I have learned that, hopefully, will be helpful to both those who lead as well as those who follow. Some of these were recorded in earlier writings during times of challenge and change.

This adventure has greatly altered my view of so many aspects of my own life and work. Often, I discovered that my marching orders from above were just the opposite from my usual actions and behavior resulting from worldly influences. It was a revelation to discover that God's definition of a *leader* is our definition of a *servant!*

—Bernie Brown

STUDY GUIDE

Most folks who write (articles, manuals, texts, books, etc.) hope that something positive will result from their efforts. My greatest desire in authoring this work is that something I will share brings meaning to something you, who read it, are doing.

If you are like me, reading is somewhat of a chore. I read slowly and my concentration capability is limited, so I generally read no more than a chapter at a time. However, some of you may be like my wife. It is not unusual for her to finish an entire book in one or two sittings. Several times I have awakened at 2:00 am to find the lights on and Snookie engrossed in a book that she could not put down. Your reading habits probably lie somewhere in between these extremes.

Irrespective of this, I have attempted to organize the book by subject matter and have included questions at the end of each chapter. The purpose of this is to stimulate deeper thinking and reflection. Therefore, it can be easily utilized as a self-study tool.

However, it also may be helpful to share your thinking and answers to the questions with others. Therefore, this format can be adapted just as effectively for group study.

In my own personal leadership development, I have participated in many study groups which proved very meaningful. The following are some suggested group settings where this material might be useful not only in sharpening leadership skills but also in fostering team-building:

1.   Leadership teams including boards, councils, committees, senior and middle management and other current and aspiring leadership groups in:
   • Businesses, companies and corporations
   • Non-profit organizations and agencies
   • Government entities
   • Educational institutions
   • Health care organizations and agencies
   • Churches and religious organizations
2.   Bible study groups, church school classes and cell groups
3.   Book review clubs
4.   Student groups including those in high school, college, graduate and continuing education programs
5.   Other interested parties

   The book has ten chapters that can easily be covered in five to ten study sessions. The questions at the end of each chapter are designed to promote further study and discussion. While this work certainly does not contain all the answers, hopefully it will raise issues in the minds and hearts of all those who read it resulting in personal growth and discovery. Again, it is but an attempt on the part of this one author to share some lessons learned while attempting to lead his organization God's way.

INTRODUCTION
COMMUNICATING THROUGH STORIES AND PARABLES

"I will open my mouth in parables, I will utter things hidden..."
—Matthew 13:35

COMMUNICATION. The mere mention of the term invokes a desire to insert "lack of" before it, thus creating a phrase that seems to be used more often than the word alone. "Lack of communication" currently receives the blame for everything from trouble at home to trouble on the job to trouble in the world. It is hard to glance through a magazine or journal of any kind without being deluged with ideas for improvement in one of man's most basic areas of need: communication with others. Included are suggestions for getting a message across and, in turn, interpreting those of others; for dealing diplomatically with coworkers in stressful situations; for communicating corporate ethics and values to those in the workplace, and on and on.

But one person's panacea for dealing with this modern problem could well be another's pitfall. It occurred to me that a *"back to the basics"* approach may be the best method to use to ensure good communication in conveying one's message.

Ronald Reagan seems to have been a master at it. Even those who had different political philosophies agreed that he was a "Great Communicator" because of his skill in presenting information using clear, easily remembered, and readily understood methods. His secret? He made heavy use of anecdotes and descriptive illustrations – parables, if you will – to convey messages and thereby created a strong bond with his audiences, most of whom could see a little of themselves in his stories.

Another person, the great teacher Confucius, also used stories and parables to illustrate moral principles to his followers. Confucius once said, "An oppressive government is more to be feared than a tiger." A mental picture of that grasping, growling tiger of a government could easily be captured in a political cartoon today – never to be forgotten.

However, the greatest storyteller of all time was a man named Jesus. His words cut across crowds of people from every walk of life because they were presented in story form and appealed to the educated and ignorant, rich and poor, rulers and slaves alike. People today can still identify with the concept of unconditional forgiveness illustrated in the parable of the prodigal son, for example. This son had disgraced his family and broken his father's heart by gambling his inheritance and frolicking his life away. Yet because he had a loving father, it was never too late for a second chance. The warm welcome home given to this wayward son by his father signified by the preparation and serving of the "Fatted Calf" is part of the language used even now in referring to the way a host welcomes guests. The fact that such stories are still remembered and meaningful more than 2,000 years later gives proof to the fact that a good story leaves a lasting impression.

Storytellers down through the ages have captivated audiences from small groups around the campfire to great crowds in arenas. Nothing can quieten a group of children like the promise of a story, and when a story is told to drive home a point, chances are the teller will not be disappointed in the results.

What does this have to do with lessons that I will share with you in the upcoming chapters? Many of these lessons, which came from experiences and observations, are presented to you in the form of stories or modern-day parables. For years, I used this communication technique within our organization and community to convey "our story."

I don't have the skills of a Ronald Reagan, the insight of a Confucius and certainly not the divine wisdom of Jesus, but I do have the desire to share a few of the **lessons I learned on the way down**. *If I remembered the story then I remembered the lesson, and if I remembered the lesson…then I could apply the principle.*

As I said, these stories largely come from my work experience, specifically in the health care field (I have found that most folks are familiar enough with hospitals, doctors and related television series to understand what I'm talking about). However, the principles they convey can be applied in any organizational setting be it large or small, for-profit or non-profit, government agency, educational institution, church, etc.

I am not a theologian. I am a practitioner in institutional leadership. Therefore, my communication style will not be scholarly but hopefully meaningful in an everyday kind of way. It is my utmost desire that you enjoy and benefit from reading the lessons I learned…on the way down.

LEADING FROM THE BOTTOM

"So the last shall be first and the first last..."
—Matthew 20:16

If you have been around executive types, you know that they love to go up to a board and draw organizational charts. It could be that a few think they have some sort of artistic talent, but I believe that most are infatuated with placing their names at the top of the charts. Being at the top can certainly be an ego inflator. I know from experience.

So, what does a good organizational structure look like? How are relationships defined? The traditional chart is typically a group of boxes stacked on top of each other in the form of a hierarchy shaped like a pyramid.

This triangular figure, which narrows at the top, primarily denotes status, influence and authority. Generally, most members of the organization strive to move upward. Promotion within such a structure implies an elevation in title and compensation. CEOs often desire to hold board memberships to enhance their positions. Department heads wish to become vice presidents, whereas vice presidents often covet the president's job. Employees work to become managers. Human nature tends to lead everyone upward and onward.

Our society promotes this in every organized setting be it a major corporation or a peewee ball team. As a young kid, I remember playing "king of the mountain," which instilled the desire in me, at a very impressionable age, to be on top of the heap. Dr. Laurence Peter, author of *The Peter Principle*, suggests that workers tend to rise to a level of incompetence before this tendency is overcome.[1] Then it is too late. They are in over their heads.

I was no different when I arrived at the top. I started drawing an organizational chart and filling in the blanks. Of course, I was at the top followed by executive VP's, senior VP's, regular VP's, assistant VP's and chiefs of about every thing you can think of. Almost as an afterthought, I placed the hard-working employees and volunteers at the bottom. Yet another level was depicted even lower on the chart – the customers/consumers of our services.

That's when I realized that I had it all wrong. I knew that, as a principle, the customers should come first. At that moment it also dawned on me that, if that was true; our frontline employees who directly delivered our services should be at the top of the chart. Our success depended far more on them than on me. Based on this revelation, I decided to do something radically different. *I flipped the organizational chart upside down.*

At the top were customers/consumers being served by frontline employees. Under them were their supervisors and managers, and toward the bottom were the executives—whose primary jobs were to support all those above. My name in the CEO's box rested at the very lowest point on the chart *at the bottom.*

I can assure you if you take this view, it is much more satisfying to look up to your folks than looking down on them. *Interestingly, the shape of this new structure is that of a highway yield sign that in itself intrinsically supports this concept.*

Some may call such a structure idealistic or Pollyanna-ish. However, in today's workplace, market forces such as competition, demand for quality services, regulations and operational efficiency are all prevalent. Therefore, new, more radical organizational approaches may be necessary. Organizational roles and relationships will be the key to success for those institutions that survive and flourish.

Maybe we *do* need to rethink our values and totally re-engineer our structures. Some have said that it is lonely at the top of an organization.

The good thing about this inverted structure is that the top is lonely no more. There are lots of folks up there.

Some might interpret this approach to leadership as actually weakening it. To the contrary, I honestly believe that leadership effectiveness is strengthened. This new organizational structure is one that inherently empowers not only the leadership but also all other levels within the structure as well. I can recall times when my authority was clearly on the line and the power necessary to fulfill my responsibilities was being threatened. Both authority and power are as important and necessary as ever. However, I have come to realize that *power* is different from *authority* because it cannot be delegated or inherited. It is a product of the possessor's own making; it is earned or acquired. Leading an organization of empowered employees can be a potent force. A leadership approach such as this should never be defined as weak, but clearly could be described (from a biblical perspective) as *meek*.

It seems to me that flipping the chart, but more importantly our mindset, upside down makes sense if we are to succeed in fulfilling the real mission of the organization – quality products and services. However, this is only the beginning. It is from this perspective that the following lessons in leadership come – from the bottom. This is why I have called this work *LESSONS LEARNED ON THE WAY DOWN!*

> **It seems to me that flipping the chart, but more importantly our mindset, upside down makes sense if we are to succeed in fulfilling the real mission of the organization – quality products and services.**

LEADERSHIP IS A GIFT

Most books on administrative theory, management and leadership do not promote the philosophy that I have just described. Is this concept a new wheel that has to be invented? No, I found it! We don't have to re-invent the wheel!

I attended a course on a unique form of leadership which exposed me to some of the most informative and helpful material that I ever received. The teacher of this class had done extensive research from the greatest book ever written on leadership, and was quite perceptive in identifying the characteristics found in effective leaders.

Being a manager high up in an organization, I once thought that I would automatically inherit the leadership role. But this is not necessarily so–there can be differences between managers and leaders. For example, managers generally focus on *control*; leaders focus on *freedom*. Management does things the right *way*; leadership does the right *thing*. Managers are *reactive*; leaders are *proactive*. In all of this, the implication is not that one is good and the other bad, but that they are different.

Leaders tend to exhibit some common traits. For example, leaders don't drive looking in the rear view mirror; they don't dwell on the past. Leaders take responsibility and don't blame others or make excuses; they feel totally accountable. Leaders don't run away from problems; they see problems as opportunities. Leaders shape the personalities of their organizations. Leaders don't boss, they serve. They help others to be the best they can be.

Finally, from this class, I learned that leadership is a gift from a higher authority. It should be exercised with much care and with a noble purpose.

I was so enthralled with the first session of this course, I went straight home to read more from the text being used by the instructor. Fortunately, I already had a copy.

> **I learned that leadership is a gift from a higher authority.**

I thanked my pastor for his great insights into leadership, extracted from this wonderful textbook—*The Holy Bible*—and began a year's study of God's view of leadership. I'm still learning. I have found it amazing how one book has the answers to so many questions, and the prescription for so many ailments!

"We have different gifts, according to the grace given us. If a man's gift is...leadership, let him govern diligently."
—Romans 12:6-8

LEADERS SHOULD TRY BEING THEIR OWN CUSTOMERS

Have you ever known an organization that did not profess to put its customers first? Yet, from my own observations, only a few actually succeed consistently. Issues such as money, personality, ego, apathy and even carelessness are among the deterrents. I have discovered that one of the best ways to regain one's perspective in this regard is to become your own customer from time to time. For the first time in years, I was required to be an inpatient in a hospital. (The last time had been when I was born.) Of course, I considered myself an expert on hospital patients since I'd worked in health care my entire adult career, but I would find I had much to learn. I was told that I would need to come into the hospital for what I'm sure was a minor and routine procedure to my doctor. However, I have now concluded that a "minor, routine procedure" can best be defined as surgery performed on someone else. This was major and not routine to me. I was literally scared to death.

I was instructed not to eat or drink anything before being admitted but when I arrived I was immediately asked to fill up a little specimen cup. That was next to impossible since I hadn't drunk anything in hours.

After surgery, one doctor told me to drink plenty so my plumbing would not shut down, and another said, "Don't drink too much or it might cause you to have a headache." (I must have drunk just the right amount because my plumbing functioned perfectly and I didn't get a headache).

I learned, too, why the little identification bracelet patients wear is made of plastic. It is so your name won't smudge when it gets wet. I sat in the bathtub so long that I looked like a prune, but my bracelet was like new. And those cute hospital gowns! Here are my thoughts about them...

First, they tie in the back so you must initially accept your dependence on others. (Someone has to tie it for you.) Secondly, they are so unattractive and unflattering; nobody will ever want to steal them. And finally, since they open in the back, I am now convinced that most hospital procedures are initiated from the rear.

I also think hospital architects should spend more time designing attractive ceilings. I found that patients look at ceilings much more than at walls and floors. The designers need to give more thought to corridors as well. When I was being rolled on a stretcher to and from the O.R.—looking straight up—I had the feeling that we were traveling through a maze. I knew the buildings, yet I was still very confused. I can imagine what others must think.

And then there's the booklet given to patients explaining about their hospital stay. I got around to it just before discharge and I was looking forward to reading it because my picture was in it. Maybe this needs to be given to patients *before* they are admitted.

What did I gain from this experience? Much relief from a health problem, an even greater appreciation for doctors and hospital personnel, and a special empathy for what patients go through. In the future, I would be more sympathetic to the pain experienced by new mothers, and I would never again snicker at folks carrying around little cushions to sit on. I became a better leader because I had the experience of being my organization's customer.

I became a better leader because I had the experience of being my organization's customer.

"I have compassion for these people..."
—Matthew 15:32

BE A SERVING LEADER

It is so easy for leaders to get into their comfort zones and forget what *"it"* is all about. This is what my wife calls *"majoring in the minors."* Perhaps what we need on a regular basis are reminders to *"major in the majors.*" I got my reminders from many sources.

As part of my regular presentation to new employees, I talked about the philosophy of serving. I usually made note of the fact that a hospital is a service organization that provides services that generally people would rather do without. This leads to the conclusion that individuals working in health care must be servants to others if the institution is to fulfill its true purpose.

This philosophy had always sounded good and noble, and the purpose of its inclusion in my orientation speech was to inspire and motivate our new personnel. However, this idea had been somewhat remote to me personally because I had become isolated and insulated while working in my big plush office. My time was filled with important meetings and conferences with board members, physician leaders and other executive types.

I regained my perspective one day when a young man asked me during an interview to define the title "administrator." I proceeded to expand upon my virtues as a leader, the many significant duties which I performed and summed it up with a description of the power and prestige I enjoyed. Then he asked this penetrating question. "From where is the word *administrator* derived?"

According to my dictionary, I discovered the base or root word is *minister*, which means to serve or care. With this revelation, the words hospital and administrator seemed to fit together better than I had ever noticed before. I was humbled by my renewed appreciation of my role as a servant. I later added this new insight concerning the definition of my title to my orientation speech. This led me to the conclusion that a service organization needs to be headed by a serving leader.

> This led me to the conclusion that a service organization needs to be headed by a serving leader.

I was in the grocery store one day after I had been retired for several years. A lady who looked somewhat familiar walked up to me and introduced herself, noting that she also had recently retired after twenty years with our hospital. She told me how much she had enjoyed her work and she shared something that was very special to me.

She said, "I will never forget your meeting with me and the other new employees and telling us that if we weren't planning to be servants, we needed to look for a job somewhere else. When I heard that, I knew it was the right place for me. The past twenty years have been a blessing."

"...whoever wants to become great among you must be your servant..."
—Matthew 20:26

LEADERSHIP IS AS MUCH AN ART AS A SCIENCE

Science is definitive; art is subjective. Are effective leaders scientists or are they artists? I believe that they are both. Certainly there are rules and defined principles but there is also much room for judgment and flexibility. I learned this at a relatively young age.

When I was in junior high, senior high and college, I worked in a grocery store on weekends, during holidays and vacations. Smith Brothers was the finest grocery and meat market in Savannah, Georgia, and those who wanted the best always shopped there. It not only had a reputation for quality, but also was considered one of the best run and most productive businesses in town.

Over the years, I became somewhat of a jack-of-all-trades. I worked in produce, frozen foods, groceries, receiving, checkout and all the different sections of the store. However, my favorite area was the meat department. I loved waiting on folks and doing all the general butchering duties. At one point, I could cut up a chicken for packaging in less time than any of the butchers. (I almost lost a finger doing that one day.)

I look back on this experience with great fondness and appreciation. I would learn many principles of management, salesmanship, finance and human relations from Messrs. Harry and Leon Smith, the owners of the store. Later, while in college and graduate school, I was exposed to many organizational theories that I had already seen in practice.

I will always remember my first day on the job there. I was a bag boy, carrying out groceries to customers' cars. A lady had purchased two cases of soft drinks which had to be brought from the back of the store. I carried one case stacked on top of another.

While trying to open the front door, I dropped both cases (48 bottles—and they were glass in those days). I will never forget this because only eight bottles survived the crash. Embarrassment, fear and humiliation all consumed me simultaneously. I didn't know whether I'd lose my job or spend my first day's income paying for those drinks.

That afternoon when I was leaving, Mr. Harry asked in a very thoughtful and interested manner how my first day on the job had gone. He never mentioned the accident, though I knew that *he* knew what a mess I had made.

Don't let me give you the wrong impression—he could really be tough at times, but he also knew when to be kind. In today's jargon, we would say that Mr. Harry's sensitivity "empowered" me to keep on trying and to believe that I could succeed. As a result, I worked my head off for those two men for the next six years. They may have had better employees but they never had a more devoted one than I.

It is amazing how a little patience, understanding and encouragement by the "big boss" can motivate an employee. That was the day it became apparent to me that leadership is as much an art as a science. My goal was always to be as good a leader as my first two bosses, Messrs. Harry and Leon Smith. (Incidentally, both of these gentlemen were outstanding hospital trustees and encouraged me to enter the field of health care administration.)

> **It became apparent to me that leadership is as much an art as a science.**

"...encourage one another daily..."
—Hebrews 3:13

PERSEVERANCE IN LEADERSHIP

Though my job as a hospital CEO sometimes seemed glamorous to outsiders, I can assure you that it was often tough! Finances could deteriorate rapidly, the competition could be intense, the politics could be vicious, and there were times I wondered, "What's a nice guy like me doing in a place like this?" However, there were also reminders that said, "It's worth it!"

I found a picture (lithograph) for which I had been looking for some time. A print of this same picture hung in the office of my first boss in the health care field.

The scene is a rocky mountain crest on which sits a single pine tree. The tree is the only vegetation at that high point on the mountain. It is deep rooted, scraggly shaped, weather worn, slightly bent and generally very unattractive. Yet it has grown tall, having weathered freezing winters and scorching summers for many years.

My former boss once indicated to me that this painting expressed his philosophy of our profession. Hospital administration is a tough job in an often hostile environment.

Some years later, after holding several other positions, I came to the realization that *all* jobs are tough, either physically and/or mentally. But this does not mean that they cannot be fulfilling. Those who do weather the storms, bend with the breeze, and persevere will in the end stand tall at the tops of their mountains.

> **Those who do weather the storms, bend with the breeze and persevere will in the end stand tall at the tops of their mountains.**

That picture hung in my office for many years as a reminder of these principles.

"Blessed is the man who perseveres under trial..."
—*James 1:12*

LEADERS HAVE TO WALK, TOO

This whole idea about flipping the chart was a good one until it came time to apply the concept. I learned quickly that it can be inconvenient but also rewarding...

Parking always seemed to be a sore point with employees, even those who parked for free. During an expansion phase at our hospital, it became a major problem because space was at a premium and people were being temporarily inconvenienced. Some even had to be shuttled to/from an off-campus lot.

I had decided several years earlier that I would give up my most convenient spot and set an example by taking the worst and furthest parking space from my office. Since I also came and went more often than most during the day, this created somewhat of a hardship for me.

One of our best, yet most vocal, employees came to my office to complain about her personal parking situation. She was leaving earlier for work and returning home later and even on occasions had to catch the shuttle. I listened with empathy and somewhat in jest said, "Let me give you my parking space!"

She lit up with a degree of amazement and said, "Do you really mean that?"

Then I shared with her my earlier decision to take the furthest space (at that time in the back of the remote lot). As she left that day, she expressed amazement that I would do such a thing. For the balance of her career with us she was one of our greatest ambassadors and a special friend.

In following this practice over the years, I received some interesting side benefits and insights. I was in much better shape physically because of my long walk at least twice a day. I still know many executives who have the closest, most convenient parking space next to their place of business. This fringe benefit is justified as a privilege of rank as well as the need to conserve executives' valuable time. However, the annual physical exams performed on these individuals often result in diagnoses of hypertensive, overweight and/or stress plagued conditions.

Ironically, the typical remedy for such problems is a fitness program which involves exercise like walking. I began to wonder why these executives didn't just park farther away from the building in the first place.

But more important than that, I discovered another reason why my remote parking space was a good thing. I was probably the least vital person in our organization when it came to expediency. In a hospital, patients must come first. I can't think of anyone they need less than the CEO at such a time.

Flipping the organizational chart is one thing; living on the bottom is another. A leader must walk the talk!

A leader must walk the talk!

"For everyone who exalts himself will be humbled, and he who humbles himself will be exalted."
—Luke 18:14

A SUPREME COMMANDMENT FOR LEADERS

I had always been big on having written rules, regulations, policies and procedures covering most everything. However, the view from the bottom of the organization caused me to reevaluate my hard stand on this.

Certainly, any large organization must have policies and procedures in order to function effectively and efficiently. But, as it grows, it seems more and more rules and regulations are promulgated. It's an organizational disease. When any new situation or problem arises, we tend to enact a new rule or regulation. (Legislative leaders are the worst at this.)

In any case, over the years, a great many policies, procedures, rules and regulations had been instituted on a formal as well as informal basis. In my office alone, there were thirty manuals dealing with general, standard and personnel policies and procedures; others with bylaws, rules and regulations for hospitals and medical staffs; plus numerous handbooks on professional groups to which I belonged. (These did not include many other books on hospital licensure and accreditation requirements and standards which must be followed in order to get a good rating.)

Conversely, anyone who has worked in an organization in which there are *no* formal policies and procedures will tell you that it is not fun to be ruled by individual whims. Yet we all know of times when we have been tripped up by our own rules even when we were trying to do the right thing. Is there an answer to this paradoxical situation? In my opinion, yes. Rules and regulations must continuously be reviewed in order to make certain that they are necessary, fair and enforced appropriately.

In addition, policies and procedures should be applied in a positive, empathetic and charitable manner, particularly those relating to the customers. In our case, patients.

While most institutional laws are necessary, there should be a supreme commandment which takes precedence. At our hospital, this commandment was *the patient comes first*. To paraphrase another rule: "Apply your rules to others as you would like them to be applied to you.

> **While most institutional laws are necessary, there should be a supreme commandment which takes precedence over all these.**

"So in everything, do to others what you would have them do to you"
—Matthew 7:12

LEADING A TEAM

College coaches are some of our most notable leaders because their effectiveness is measured immediately and continuously. Their records are visible to all. One of my favorite people in the world of sports was the legendary Paul "Bear" Bryant, who retired as coach of the Crimson Tide of the University of Alabama, only to die unexpectedly a few weeks later. At the time, Coach Bryant was the winningest coach in college football history, with 323 wins over a 38-year career. I developed a long-standing interest in Bear Bryant because I once had the opportunity to meet him. While a lowly administrative resident at the University of Alabama Medical Center, I was asked to attend a president/faculty reception for someone who did not want to take time to go. After arriving, I walked around the beautiful presidential mansion feeling very insignificant and out-of-place. I entered a room and bumped right into Coach Bryant. As we shook hands he said, "I'm Paul Bryant," to which I replied, "I'm Bernie Brown. Glad to meet you." That was about the extent of our conversation.

I'll always remember this encounter, and I would like to think that Mr. Bryant remembered meeting this young, impressive, aspiring hospital administration student.

We can learn a great deal by observing the methods, techniques and principles used by highly successful individuals. One source for me would be Coach Bryant's comments after his last game in the Liberty Bowl, which incidentally, Alabama won.

His first words were in praise of his assistant coaches and players. He went so far as to say that he personally had had very little to do with the win that day and reiterated that which he had stated so often: "The key to a winning team is not the head coach's play calling but instead his recruitment and selection of outstanding assistant coaches and players and letting them do their jobs."

Every team member has something to contribute and, if given the right opportunity and encouragement, will do so with flying colors. Coach Bryant knew that his assistant coaches and players were more important than he was. He placed himself *at the bottom of the chart.*

> **Every team member has something to contribute and, if given the right opportunity and encouragement, will do so with flying colors.**

A few other thoughts concerning the "Bear": The fall after our meeting, Coach Bryant started at quarterback a rebellious young kid who refused to wear socks on campus. His name was Joe Willie Namath and he led Alabama to a national championship that year. Finally, my real name is "Bernard," which according to Webster's Dictionary, means "bold as a bear." Maybe my accidental encounter with Coach Paul "Bear" Bryant was not an accident after all.

"…many advisors make victory sure."
—Proverbs 11:14

To further emphasize the importance of leadership in team effectiveness, let me share with you the thinking of another of the great sports leaders of the twentieth century. He stated…"I truly realize that (my organization) is made up of as many different individuals as there are positions in it; that some need a whip and others a pat on the back; and others are better off when they are ignored; and that there are limitations imposed by the difference in physical ability and mentality. The amount that can be consumed and executed by the team is controlled by the weakest man in it, and while others can give him physical help, he has to do his own thinking." [2]

Treating team members as individuals is an important principle for winning. In this case, the organization was the former World Champion Green Bay Packers and the leader was Coach Vince Lombardi.

> **Treating team members as individuals is an important principle for winning.**

"…but God disciplines us for our good, that we may share in his holiness."
—Hebrews 12:10

DISCIPLINING A LEADER

Leading from the bottom allows others within the organization to view you differently. Instead of seeing themselves and you in a traditional superior/subordinate relationship, they tend to consider you more as a supporter and an enabler. As a result, they may even feel freer to give you helpful guidance and counsel. The following describes such an encounter.

I was disciplined the other day. Or to put it another way, "my hand was spanked" for doing something that was wrong. Obviously, we all make mistakes; we err in judgment or at times put our mouths in gear before engaging our brains. Often our wrongdoings are innocent, without malice or prejudice, but sometimes we just don't have our heads on straight and do things intentionally which later prove to be downright stupid.

But I do not want to dwell on mistakes and poor judgments. Instead, I want to tell you what I learned from the person who disciplined me. I had said something that offended some members of our staff, and needed not only to be corrected but also warned not to repeat that particular mistake.

The counseling session following my transgression started on a very positive note. I was initially told that I generally do a good job, and don't make many errors in judgment. This was positive reinforcement and helped me retain some self-esteem. Then it was pointed out to me that I had really "screwed this up" and "blown it." This left no doubt in my mind that I had done something wrong and needed to straighten up. But he didn't leave me there. His next move was to give me some pointers on how to effectively address such a situation should it arise again.

I had always heard that this was a good approach to use when disciplining a person. First, say something good about the person, then make sure that he or she knows exactly what you mean when citing that which is bad, and last, offer some positive suggestions for improvement. After the session, I felt good and bad at the same time.

I knew that I had worth to the organization, but I needed to do better in the future to add to my value and effectiveness. Viewing this retrospectively, there is no doubt in my mind that I am now a better person because I was disciplined in such a meaningful manner.

I will always be grateful that I had working for me individuals with the maturity, integrity, honesty and guts to come in, close the door and discipline their boss when he needed it. Discipline is as good for the soul of a leader as for a follower.

> **Discipline is as good for the soul of a leader as for a follower.**

"Whoever loves discipline loves knowledge, but he who hates correction is stupid."
—Proverbs 12:1

BEING A POPULAR LEADER

In making the shift from the top to the bottom of the organization, the change in one's mindset can create some personal problems. For example, the human craving for popularity and public praise must be tempered. I have continuously struggled with this tendency but have finally reconciled it in my own mind.

Being a popular administrator was tough. Yet, I surely did like being liked. It really pumped me up when someone said something nice about me, and on the other hand, my feelings were hurt when something negative was directed my way. I guess this desire to be liked goes back to my younger days. Like most children and youth, popularity was quite important to me and to be honest, this need still exists.

When I was older and got a job, I first decided the way to be popular was to please those with whom I worked. In other words, if I could just say and do the things that would make others happy, I knew they would like me. After only a short period, I ran into problems with that philosophy. I remember telling one person what he wanted to hear to make him happy, and then telling another person just the opposite to make her feel good. This worked fine until the two of them got together and compared notes. They were totally confused about my position on that particular issue, and I soon didn't know where I stood either.

On other occasions, I probably distorted the truth a little because I didn't want to say something that would make me unpopular. At times, I even dishonestly agreed with those who had different points of view just to avoid conflict. I'm sure this tended to befuddle those around me, and as a result I lost their approval anyway.

After discovering that being a "yes person" didn't win me popularity, I decided that perhaps total honesty and straightforwardness was the answer. In using this approach, I felt better about myself, but I tended to clash with others because of my dogmatic stance and inflexible attitude on many issues. I became somewhat of a rebel and as a result, my popularity waned considerably.

Then I thought maybe I could just eliminate such unpleasantness by totally avoiding critical problems and undesirable situations. This way I would not have to face any circumstances which required an unpopular stand. That didn't work either, because the problems in my area remained unsolved, and my credibility went down the tubes.

What was the answer? Should I give up the desire to be liked? Was it impossible for a hospital administrator to be popular? I hoped not. It would probably be unnatural for one not to want approval, compassion and respect from others. But maybe there was a better way to gain real popularity.

When I began viewing this differently, I realized that the people I liked best were often folks who were *not* seeking popularity. Sometimes they even disagreed with me, yet did so in a tactful manner. In fact, they were not trying to be anyone but themselves. As a result, I started trying to be more like those I liked. I realized that popularity is only meaningful if it results from being one's true self. Being popular is now much further down on my priority list.

> **I realized that popularity is only meaningful if it results from being one's true self.**

"Do not think of yourself more highly than you ought…"
—*Romans 12:3*

AFFIRMATION

It worked! Every once and awhile something happens which lets you know that what you are trying to do is working. In this case, a front-line worker proved that he could function much better than I could at the top of the organization. I had just received a call informing me that I had been selected as one of the 100 most influential and powerful persons in Georgia. There was to be a luncheon to recognize me and the other ninety-nine, which included a past president, governor, senators, congressmen and many business and community leaders. I had never been before (nor since) in such "high cotton."

The luncheon was great. I sat beside the CEO of a Fortune 500 company. After some small talk, he asked me what I did (I knew what he did). I proudly told him that I had been the CEO of Kennestone Hospital in Marietta for many years which was now a large health system. I braced myself to acknowledge the admiration and accolades which I anticipated from this person for my achievements. He paused for a second and exclaimed, "That's great! You work at Fred's hospital!" I thought, "What are you talking about? That's Bernie's hospital!" Then he went on to share experiences he had had at our hospital and how helpful Fred, our security officer in the parking lot, had been to him.

Sadly, later that year, I attended the funeral of a good man and a true friend named Fred Rohner. The preacher, while giving the eulogy, made the observation that probably all those in attendance had been helped by this man in finding a parking place at Kennestone Hospital. Most smiled and acknowledged that this was true. Family and friends of patients at this large, busy hospital came and went constantly and most had been greeted by this friendly gentleman who had only one good eye.

I sat there and felt special because "I worked at Fred's hospital." That's right; I worked at Fred's hospital. I also worked at Janie's, Gloria's, Linda's, Myrtle's, Ursula's, Lisa's, Shirley's, Dorothy's, Emily's, Bobbie's, Pete's, Rene's, Vi's, Sharon's, Carolyn's, Janelle's, Claire's, Charlie's, Marcia's, Ann's, Lena's, Grace's, Sara's, Beverly's, Tony's, Debra's, Buddy's, Pearl's, Tom's, Jane's, Joe's, Denye's, Louise's, Betty's, Doris's, Kaye's, Mary Ann's, Donna's, Saundra's, Jeanne's, John's, Alta's, Toni's...hospital, too.

In thinking about Fred and the many others like those listed above, I have concluded that they truly believed that their jobs were necessary to the success of the organization. They continuously felt this way because their supervisors, department directors and senior managers reinforced that belief in them.

If you have ever observed frontline workers who felt the importance of their jobs, you know what I mean when I say that the organizational chart needs to be turned upside down. It is much more fun leading from the bottom. I could feel the joy of seeing the achievements of the thousands at the top!!

It is much more fun leading from the bottom.

Because I knew Fred Rohner personally, there is no doubt in my mind that he is helping folks find a parking place up in heaven right now. I just hope that it is as crowded up there as it was in our parking lots down here.

"Whatever you do, work at it with all your heart..."
—Colossians 3:23

LEADING FROM THE BOTTOM

"So the last shall be first and the first last..."
—Matthew 20:16

Questions for Further Study and Discussion

1. Is flipping the organizational chart a literal or symbolic decision? Would such a concept work in a highly structured and regimented organization such as the military?

2. If leadership is a gift, who bestows it? Who allows one to exercise the gift?

3. If its leaders become an organization's customers will they be treated differently? If possible, should a leader do so incognito? Are all organizations service-oriented? Can organizations work just as well without a serving leader?

4. If leadership is as much an art as a science, can one who is primarily an artist be an effective leader? Can one who is primarily a scientist be an effective leader?

5. Are some jobs tougher than others? How important is perseverance?

6. Can a leader just "talk" without "walking" and still be effective? Is there anything wrong with a preferential parking place (and all it implies)?

7. How important are formal policies and procedures? Can you periodically "bend the rules" without repercussions?

8. Should a leader treat every team member the same? How do you motivate individuals to be team players? Would you have the guts to discipline your boss? How would you approach it?

9.   Is popularity necessary for good leadership? Are you true to yourself in your job?

10. How important is affirmation in leadership? Who should affirm whom?

ORGANIZATION OR ORGANISM

"For the body is not one member, but many."
—1 Corinthians 12:14

As a leader in an institutional setting, I was constantly trying to understand the nature of the environment in which I worked. In my mind, this was essential if I was to be effective as a leader. I gained insight one day from a child.

Some years ago, one of our employees told me about an incident that occurred when her young son was in elementary school. During a science lesson, the students were asked if they knew what an "organism" was. Tommy was first to raise his hand. He answered, "My Mom works at one—the Kennestone *organism*." (Of course, he was thinking of the Kennestone Hospital *organization*). I remember laughing and suggesting that this should be sent to *Reader's Digest*.

Every time I recall this little story, I am amused, yet amazed. In a sense, I considered it an innocent Freudian slip. It raised an interesting question: Is a hospital an organization, or is it an organism? My thesaurus indicates that an organization is a company or business establishment—a functional structure. An organism is a living being or creature. Interestingly, organization and organism have the same base. The root word is *organ*. An organ is a body part performing a function or cooperating with others in an activity. An organ is a component of every organization and the basis of every organism.

Why am I carrying you through this exercise in semantics? Maybe it's because a significant principle is involved here. We as individuals are the organs which jointly make up a functional yet dormant structure called an organization. However, an organization that is merely a structure cannot be effective. In addition, it must become a living, breathing creature – an organism. Unless an organization becomes an organism, it will lack energy, motivation, dedication, enthusiasm and all the other attitudinal characteristics which lead to success.

> **Unless an organization becomes an organism, it will lack energy, motivation, dedication, enthusiasm and all the other attitudinal characteristics which lead to success.**

It seemed to me that Tommy was right. His mom did work for the Kennestone organism. I was thankful that we were so blessed with good people (organs), who made that hospital such a great organization. We truly were a body made up of many members (organs).

AN ORGANIZATIONAL FAMILY

I often wondered how best to promote an environment of mutual respect and cooperation among the staff. In this regard, I desired to create a family atmosphere, but soon learned that those at the top were much better at creating it than I was at the bottom.

Many times I referred to our people as a "hospital family." We tended to use this term most often at employee activities such as award nights, birthday parties, retirement receptions , etc. At one of those occasions, I discovered just what hospital family really means.

A 15-year employee named Mildred was retiring. After I had made my brief presentation at the reception in her honor, I asked if anyone else had anything to say. A younger lady named Ruby came up to pay tribute to her "mother" by expressing what Mildred had meant to her and the hospital over the years. I was so impressed by what she said that I made a point to talk with her later. She told me this story:

Mildred started to work in the nursery in 1967 and shortly afterward Ruby was employed in the same area. They became very good friends and on a Mother's Day, Ruby sent Mildred a card. Mildred was touched but saddened since she had never had any children of her own. Upon learning this, Ruby, who had lost her mother earlier, said, "I'll be your daughter if you will 'adopt' me."

So a mother-daughter relationship began. Over the years, the love and respect between these two individuals grew and many of our own people knew about and were inspired by this unique relationship.

It is interesting to observe adopted parents and children together. It seems to me that as time goes on, some of the mannerisms, characteristics, personalities and even their looks become similar though they are not actually blood kin. Such was the case of Mildred and Ruby.

That day I had my picture taken with the two of them at the reception because I felt such a part of their "hospital family." What made the photo and story behind it even more significant was the fact that Mildred Byrd, the mother, was white; her "daughter" Ruby Robinson was black.

I was reminded that day that family is not something you just talk about. It is something you do. My mother taught me that lesson many years ago, not by what she said, but by what she did. My organizational family really came alive for me that day.

> **I was reminded that day that family is not something you just talk about. It is something you do.**

"...Here is your mother..."
—*John 19:27*

THE IMPORTANCE OF PURPOSE

I learned early on that unhappy, dissatisfied, disgruntled employees are not only non-productive but often disruptive within the organization. Was there anything that I could do from my lowly perch to positively influence these folks?

From time to time, I read or hear that the majority of people are unhappy in their jobs. I interpret this to mean that these individuals either don't like what they are doing or they don't like where they are employed or they don't like those with whom they work. This is very sad to me personally; I must have been one in the minority because I loved what I did, I loved where I was employed and I loved those with whom I had the privilege of working.

In this regard, I once observed a full page ad in a local newspaper which was evidently purchased by an individual. It was entitled "A Personal Message of Thanks for Some Very Fine People." After 36 years of employment, a pilot for a major airline was retiring and chose to use this unusual method to thank many people for their contributions to his career. He evidently was happy in his job.

I have often wondered why some are so happy yet others so extremely unhappy while working side by side in an organization. Could it be individual circumstances? No; at times folks with the most difficult personal and professional situations seem to be the happiest, while those who appear to have it all going their way are the unhappiest.

Could it be pay and benefits? No, sometimes the people making the least are the happiest, while those who have trouble deciding how to spend all their income are unhappy.

Could it be environment or heredity? No, no, no. Nothing like that. Then what could it be? Many psychological studies and analyses have been conducted to determine the reasons, and many seminars and classes have been held in an attempt to explain the reasons. Therefore, I may be somewhat presumptuous in trying to offer a simple solution to this complex riddle.

As a member of the happy minority, it seems to me that it all boils down to one basic reason. The happy employee (or any person for that matter) has a *purpose*, and the unhappy one does not. One of the happiest volunteers I ever knew was a cancer victim whose purpose was to help other cancer patients. One of the happiest employees I knew had as her purpose clean, beautiful rooms for patients. One of the happiest doctors I knew probably worked some of the longest hours for the least pay. His purpose was the treatment of sick children.

The happiest administrator I knew was one who attended a lot of boring meetings, who often got bogged down in daily paperwork, who was called on to perform many undesirable tasks and who seemed to be constantly changing and stripping his gears because of the complexity of his organization. His goal was to run the best health care system in the world.

There is a sad part of this little story. The happy minority could easily become the vast majority if only individuals could discover their purposes. You see, each of us has a purpose. Thank God for that!

> **The happy minority could easily become the vast majority if only individuals could discover their purposes.**

By the way, a full page ad at that time cost around $7,000. Joseph H. Moss, an airline pilot, used this means to thank his friends for helping him fulfill his purpose, and I know he feels it was worth every penny.

(This note came a few weeks after this story appeared in our institution's newsletter: "Dear Bernie, 'Thanks for your kind comments. You're correct. It was worth every cent. I'd gladly paid more.' Best to you, Joe Moss.")

"...who have been called according to his purpose..."
—Romans 8:28

MOVING DOWN THE LADDER

Once in a while employees asked me, "How can I get a promotion and advance in the organization?" Their goal was to move up the ladder. I'm certain that my answers in the beginning were inadequate because I was usually caught off guard and had not given it much thought. However, in time I came up with the following suggestions which I feel are still applicable for today:

- Be selective. In a multi-disciplined organization such as ours, you should aspire to positions for which you have the formal credentials. Therefore, you should determine what your training and experience qualifies you to do.

• Be on the team. In your current job, you must prove yourself a team member. You may be the greatest in the world at what you do, but if your supervisor and department head don't consider you on their team, your chances for bigger and better things are poor.

• Be loyal with honesty. If you cannot be loyal to your supervisor, change jobs. I personally always considered the loyalty of the people working with me to be as necessary as competence.

• Be aggressive but not offensive. You need to make your mark, but not by alienating others.

• Be persistent. You will fail many times in reaching your goals. Do a post-mortem on your efforts and determine where you fell short, and then try again.

• Finally, if you choose to climb the organizational ladder, I wish you well. However, remember in an organization that has been turned upside down, you will be climbing downward. Do not let this discourage you, for great satisfaction awaits those who descend.

> **Remember in an organization that has been turned upside down, you will be climbing downward. Do not let this discourage you, for great satisfaction awaits those who descend.**

"...his work will be shown for what it is..."
—*1 Corinthians 3:13*

THE IMPORTANCE OF ENCOURAGEMENT

In any organization, encouragement is important. In an upside down organism, encouragement is a way of life. I was always proud when I saw members of our staff encouraging one another. Here is an account of an incident that was exemplary of this.

We had some good tattle-tales around our hospital. A regular run-of-the-mill tattle-tale is one who spreads negative tales or gossip that hurts someone. A good tattle-tale is one who discloses a true story which uplifts everyone. Let me share a note I received from one of my good tattle-tail friends.

"Do we have a hidden hero award or designation? Amidst all the technical, clinical and administrative tangles you confront, I've been impressed with your everyday, people-oriented observations of life at our hospital. Because of your regard for people who go beyond the required, or whose attitude is exemplary, I would like to share with you a nomination for a hidden hero award.

While waiting in the hall for an elevator the other day, I witnessed an interaction between a young girl with cancer, an RN and the volunteer pushing the stuffed animal/vending cart. The young girl was quite ill and frail and was standing with her mother in the doorway of her room when the cart came by. As she looked at the stuffed animals, the nurse approached and they pulled down a couple of animals and talked about them. The girl's eyes couldn't hide her pleasure over one droopy-eyed puppy. The nurse asked if she liked the puppy, and she nodded, smiling. Without hesitation, the nurse pulled the price tag off the puppy and told the girl the puppy could be hers. For a long moment, it seemed, the girl grasped the puppy and held it closely as she rocked it back and forth—a brief respite of warmth and comfort from her struggle with illness. The nurse waited for the girl to move back into the room and asked the volunteer to payroll-deduct the cost of the puppy from her next paycheck.

I was touched by the nurse's sensitivity and expression of caring. Maybe staff shouldn't get so involved with patients, but as I reflected on this nurse's actions, I couldn't think of anything but good. I would like to nominate this nurse as a hidden hero!"

I thanked Becca for being such a good tattle-tale. She was special because she wanted her co-worker recognized as a hidden hero. I also sent a special thank-you and commendation to Margaret for caring so personally. In my mind, encouraging ranks right up there with caring.

> **In my mind encouraging ranks right up there with caring.**

I was blessed to be associated with an organization made up of so many encouraging, caring people. I made it known that if anyone ever wanted to tattle to me about a colleague (good tattling, I mean), my ears were always open.

"My purpose is that they may be encouraged..."
—*Colossians 2:2*

THE NEED FOR UNDERSTANDING AND HARMONY

I love music. Over the years I have learned a great many organizational lessons from participating in and observing musical groups. When everything is together, the result can be beautiful, but it can be really bad when things are not.

Over the years, it has been one of my great pleasures in life to sing in church choirs. My wife also sang, so this was an activity we enjoyed together. I remember an occasion which taught me the need for clarity and understanding.

We were practicing a beautiful new anthem, and I must say, I thought we were doing a superb job. The blend was good, the dynamics were effective, and we were all on pitch. When we finished the piece, we exchanged glances of satisfaction and then looked expectantly at our director, waiting for the praise we felt we had earned. "That was beautiful," he said. "The only problem was I couldn't understand a word you sang."

Somehow that reminded me a bit of us. We were an organization made up of good people; we believed we were doing the right things to improve our community's health; we knew we were on the cutting edge of innovation and leadership in preparing our organization for the changes that were constant assailing us. But, there were people out there who didn't understand a word we were saying! When the song is familiar, the listener can follow the words without too much trouble. However, we were singing a brand-new song, and unless we could get our message across clearly, we would have failed to gain the desired appreciation and support among those we serve. A new song (change) requires great clarity to insure understanding.

> **Change requires great clarity to insure understanding.**

At the time, I thought when we were called upon to sing our song, our 18,000 member choir needed to really concentrate on the words!

"Sing to him a new song…"
—*Psalm 33:3*

Understanding is important, but harmony is also essential. As I mentioned, I tend to look for lessons in the many different situations I observe. At times, there is possibly little to be learned, but it's always interesting to view experiences in this manner.

Once I attended a junior high school year-end band concert. One of the several bands playing that evening had just begun its last and most difficult piece. As it started, there seemed to be some very unusual chords and combinations. What I thought was to be a somewhat classical, beautiful melody seemingly turned out to be one of those modern, contemporary, weird-sounding compositions.

Then abruptly, the band director stopped moving his baton and tapped on the lectern. He stepped off the riser and in front of everybody said in a soft, yet distinct voice, "We can do better than that." I surmised that certain sections of the band were "off pitch and out of sync" and the longer they played, the more discord, disharmony and conflict were created.

This very capable director then raised his baton and started over. With a new beginning and renewed confidence and concentration on the part of the musicians, this piece of music became one of the best performed that evening.

Now the lessons! It seemed to me that there were several. First, if you get off on the wrong foot, stop and start over. Second, don't be embarrassed to recognize failure. Third, concentrate on what you are doing. However, the most important lesson is this. If we do not play (work) in harmony with one another, the organization will not succeed.

> **If we do not work in harmony with one another, the organization will not succeed.**

Band concerts are not usually my favorite way to spend an evening. However, I enjoyed this one tremendously and look forward to other learning experiences like this.

"Live in harmony with one another."
—Romans 12:16

EVALUATING HUMAN ASSETS

Just how valuable are the people who work for an organization? Other assets are evaluated regularly and methodically, but what about the people?

At the end of each fiscal year, I usually reviewed the year-end financial statements and audit with Glenn Black, our long term chief financial officer, and other members of the Financial Affairs Division. It was always interesting to note the changes which had occurred during the course of a particular year. Our financial people would point out that some of our assets had increased due to appreciation and some had decreased in value because of depreciation. Probably the most dramatic example of changing values was reflected in the need to annually increase our insurance coverage because the replacement cost of our facilities had risen so significantly.

Out of curiosity, I once asked Glenn why some things appreciated (grew in value), while others depreciated (lessened in value). He told me that there were many factors that affected the worth of an asset, but in short, he noted, "Things that get better with age appreciate, while those that get worse depreciate in value."

At the time this statement made me ask myself, "As an employee, who seemed to be aging rapidly, was I an appreciating or a depreciating asset to our organization?" We generally don't think of people in those terms, but when measuring the organization's effectiveness, no doubt our greatest assets are our employees. Therefore, the question was certainly pertinent.

In a free enterprise system such as ours, the value of a commodity is generally determined by the law of supply and demand. If an item is somewhat scarce and/or there is a great desire to have that item, then its value increases and appreciation results.

Conversely, the opposite is also true in the marketplace. In an organization which has service as its primary purpose, here are a few of the ingredients which make a person appreciate or increase in value:

- Personal character and integrity
- Common purpose with an organization
- Positive attitude
- Rising level of competence
- Ability to grow and handle change.

It seems to me that the value of any asset (whether it is a building, a piece of equipment or a person) never remains static. It either appreciates or depreciates. In the case of people, the value is largely determined by the efforts of the individual. Those persons who consciously exert continuous effort toward those ingredients listed above will be in great demand by any organization. And remember, God places his greatest value on people.

> **God places his greatest value on people.**

Hopefully, we can all make the same claim as that aging philosopher who once stated, "I ain't getting older; I'm getting better."

"And how much more valuable you are…"
—Luke 12:24

GENERATING ENTHUSIASM

How do you get your folks enthusiastic about their work and their organization? I have reached the conclusion that enthusiasm is somewhat like a contagious disease. If you are around someone who has it, you are bound to get it. I learned this at an Atlanta Braves game.

In Atlanta, we all have our memories of the National League Playoffs and the World Series in which our Atlanta Braves played during the past fourteen years. One year, I bought tickets and was able to attend four of the six games held in Atlanta. Members of my family took turns going to the games and sat in the same seats between third base and home plate each night. In addition to the most exciting baseball games I have ever seen, the thing that I remember most was the lady who sat next to us at all the games. Her name was Arlene, and she was a very personable individual who waved a mean red hand-crafted tomahawk.

The first thing that impressed me about Arlene was the fact that she kept score using the printed program. I mean, she knew how to record each play. It was obvious that she was quite knowledgeable about the game and was an ardent Braves fan. In our initial conversations, we discovered that she was a special education supervisor in a large high school and taught some classes at the college level. Her interest in baseball was generated from the fact that her father had been a minor league player when she was a child. As she put it, "I have a passion for baseball, the Braves and particularly for my hero, John Smoltz." She wore a button with his picture on it every night.

Arlene was a real student of the game. When I was constantly second guessing the manager's decisions, she would explain his strategy to me. When things were going badly, she remained positive and optimistic. She seemed to understand not only the fundamentals, but also the psychology of the game. But what endeared her most to us was her enthusiasm and support for the Atlanta Braves.

She said that she had attended 17 Braves games that year, all against the Mets and Phillies. Then she had decided to extend herself and buy tickets to the World Series.

Each game I looked forward to seeing Arlene to hear her analysis and enjoy her contagious enthusiasm. I thought to myself, "If I could bottle Arlene's spirit and bring it back to share with others, what an impact it would have. If we as individuals could be as loyal, committed and positive as Arlene was toward baseball and the Braves, it seemed to me that our potential for effective and productive living would be almost unlimited." I learned from Arlene that enthusiasm is contagious because I caught it from her at those games.

> **I learned that enthusiasm is contagious because I caught it.**

As we gave each other "high fives" and hugs after the last home game (the Braves prevailed 14-5), I was a little sad because we would probably never see our friend Arlene again. She left immediately so she could get a head start back to her home—in New Jersey!

"...your enthusiasm has stirred most of them to action."
—2 Corinthians 9:29

BEING AN EXAMPLE

In an organizational setting which emphasizes the importance of front-line employees, the existence of good role models is a necessity.

These are individuals who serve as exceptional examples of commitment to their work and support of the institution. Such folks are often found in unexpected places.

One of the fringe benefits of being the CEO of a large institution was having the opportunity to personally meet a lot of very nice, and sometimes even famous, people. For example, I have met with heads of other major organizations, several movie and television stars, some professional athletes, many national, state and local legislators, and a number of renowned professionals, including doctors, lawyers, ministers, educators, coaches, artists and authors. I have been in the offices of six governors and even shook hands with one President of the United States. But I probably received my greatest thrill when, after a Hospice gala, my wife and I and two other couples had the privilege of having dessert with Miss America.

I want to share with you a little story told by Kaye Lani Rae Rafko, Miss America of 1988, who incidentally is an oncology nurse. It not only demonstrates the type of person she is, but also conveys what is truly important in life. Naturally, I can't tell this as well as she did, so bear with me.

Kaye Lani first pointed out that the title of "Miss America" is one of the most recognized titles in the world. It opens many doors for the one who holds it. She cited several examples of the glamour and privileges which accompany this title. Then she told about a visit to an elementary school where she met with a second grade class. The students were full of questions about what it's like to be Miss America and they also wanted to know about her personally.

Later, a parent offered some interesting feedback. At home that evening, one of the girls said to her mother, "I met Miss America today, and I'm going to be Miss America when I grow up." Of course, like any proud parent, the mother encouraged her, but pointed out how she would need to maintain her beauty, nurture her talents and develop her poise. To all of this, the little girl answered, "I want to be Miss America —I want to be a nurse!"

That night it seemed to me that the nurses I have known are a lot like Miss America. They have beautiful qualities about them that go more than skin deep. They have developed certain skills and talents that make them indispensable to a hospital. And they exhibit great poise under circumstances that are often very difficult. It is wonderful and necessary to have great examples and role models for our people.

> **It is wonderful and necessary to have great examples and role models for our people.**

As we walked out of the restaurant that night, I couldn't help but whisper to the waiter, "That was Miss America. She's a nurse!"

"In everything set them an example by doing what is good"
—*Titus 2:7*

ROOM TO GROW WITH ROOTS INTERTWINED

There seem to be some "natural" laws that have application in organizational settings. It is interesting how truth is constant wherever it is found – in this case both in the forest and in the workplace.

We all need room to grow. I'm told that children develop best when they are given some controlled independence. I've heard when students are stymied by teachers, their interests and creativity suffer. I believe that one's spouse needs to feel that he or she is not being crowded or smothered too much, or the marriage relationship is adversely affected.

Room to grow is a natural law, for it can be observed in many different settings. Let me give you an example. When we moved into this area in the early seventies, the builder had cleared only about fifteen feet behind our new house, so most of the backyard was a jungle of trees, wild bushes and vines. As we settled in, I started clearing the rest of the yard and planting grass. In the area where I was working, I discovered a small cedar tree which was only about one foot tall. It appeared almost dead from the weight of the strangling encroachers and the lack of nurturing sunlight. As I dug, pulled and mowed the underbrush, I staked this little tree to save it

Once freed from the burden of overcrowding and a smothering environment, the little tree stated to grow. When we moved, almost twenty years later, that cedar tree was approximately twenty-five feet tall, and every year it housed a robin's nest.

Room to grow is also an organizational law; to stand still is to lose ground in today's world. We were fortunate at our hospital to be part of a vital, thriving community that fostered growth of our organization. It would have been hard not to grow during those years. Like the cedar tree in my backyard, the institution had room to develop into a strong tree with room on its branches for many "nests" of service for our community. Organizations, as well as individuals, need room to grow.

> **Organizations as well as individuals need room to grow.**

"I planted the seed...watered it, but God made it grow."
—1 Corinthians 3:6

Another lesson from nature: During some storms which hit our area, we lost more than twenty trees in the yard. A tornado passed directly through our backyard uprooting several of the largest ones. Then two weeks later, the rest of the trees, which evidently were weakened by the high winds and torrential rain, were felled by a rare blizzard.

Interestingly, all but two of the downed trees were pines and those two were crushed because they were directly in line with the falling pine trees. None of the other gum or hardwood trees were affected. This experience led me to wonder: "Why do pine trees fall so easily?"

Some informal research led me to discover that some types of trees are far more stable than others. Some can endure wind, rain, cold and the other adverse conditions, while others succumb easily. I learned that pine trees are probably the least durable and redwoods the most durable in this regard.

What is the primary difference between the endurance of the tall, slender pine and that of the giant, mammoth redwood? Despite the fact that both are considered soft woods and are used extensively in construction, a basic difference exists that could cause the first to easily break and fall and the other to almost never yield to the elements. That characteristic is the root system. The pine has a primary tap root which grows straight down to give stability to the tree. The depth of this root can often be very shallow if it meets any resistance such as hard soil or rock. Therefore, when pressure is applied, the tree can become unstable. In contrast, the redwood has a very large and wide root system. Furthermore, because it primarily grows in a forest of redwoods, its roots become intermingled with other trees. As a result one tree adds stability to the others. In other words, an interdependence develops as a result of the relationship among the root systems.

The discovery of this truth was important to me because I went through awful storms from time to time in my job, as well as in my life in general. Tornadoes resulting from conflict and turmoil have passed directly over me several times. Could it be that the only reason I am still standing straight and tall is the fact that I have been supported and sustained by those close to me?

To this day, I am thankful for family, friends and associates who have kept me stable because they had their roots intertwined with mine. Hopefully, I have had a similar influence on them as they have encountered the storms of life.

> **I am thankful for family, friends and associates who have kept me stable because they had their roots intertwined with mine.**

"But since he has no root, he lasts only a short time.
—Matthew 13:21

A KEY MEMBER OF THE ORGANIZATION

How often in organizations have we heard, "It is important to have everyone on the same page!" I would take it a step further; on that page everyone must do his or her part. Otherwise, the entire enterprise can be adversely affected and the organization's message lost. Here is an illustration:

I was one of the last hold-outs to get a personal computer on my desk at work. However, after re-reading this little essay typed on my old typewriter, I became a convert to the age of technology and spell-check!

"Though my typxwrtxr is an old modxl, it works vxry wxll, xcxpt for onx of thx kxys. I havx wishxd many timxs that it workxd pxrfxctly, but it doxsn't, as you can sxx. It is trux that thxrx arx 45 kxys on this typxwritxr that function, but just onx not working makxs a big diffxrxncx. Somxtimxs it sxxms to mx that our organization is somxwhat likx my old typxwrixr – not all thx mxmbxrs arx working propxrly. You may say to yoursxlf, 'Wxll, I am only onx mxmbxr. Whxthxr I work or not will not makx or brxak thx organization.' But it doxs makx a diffxrancx, bxcausx an organization, to bx xffxc-tivx, nxxds thx activx participation of xvxry mxmbxr. So, thx nxxt timx you think you arx only onx mxmbxr and your xf-forts arx not nxxdxd, rxmxmbxr my old typxwritxr and say to yoursxlf, 'I am a kxy mxmber of this hxalth systxm and I am nxxdxd vxry much. I will do what I can.'"

Keys are essential to the opening of locked doors to houses, but more importantly, to the gates leading to knowledge and understanding. A key to an organization's success is a clear message of service and care delivered collectively by all its members.

> **A key to an organization's success is a clear message of service and care delivered collectively by all its members.**

"I will give you the keys of the kingdom of heaven…"
—*Matthew 16:19*

ORGANIZATION OR ORGANISM

"For the body is not one member, but many..."
—*1 Corinthians 12:14*

Questions for Further Study and Discussion

1. Is the concept of organization/organism useful?

2. Can organizational families survive in today's complex society? Can an organization and its workers (organs) be loyal to one another?

3. Is your organization's purpose well defined and understood? Is your personal purpose consistent with that of the organization?

4. Does the concept of moving down the ladder instead of up discourage personal initiative and aspiration?

5. Is the atmosphere in your organization one of encouragement? Who generally encourages whom?

6. Are your institution's mission, plans and objectives clear and understood? Does harmony exist generally throughout the organization?

7. Are programs in place in your organization assisting its people to appreciate rather than depreciate in value? Which way is your personal value to the organization going?

8. Is enthusiasm alive and contagious? If not, what should be done?

9. Are there good role models throughout your organization?

10. Do people feel that they have room to grow? Is there a sense of interdependence among the staff which fosters mutual support?

11. Remember the bad typewriter key? Are there one or more who either blur or ruin your organization's message?

PROFESSIONALLY WE SERVE, PERSONALLY WE CARE

"Where there is no vision, the people perish..."
—Proverbs 29:18 KJV

We needed a slogan for our organization. We were experiencing tremendous growth, and I was afraid that we might lose that special attitude and atmosphere we had enjoyed as a smaller institution. As the organization's leader, I believed it was my responsibility to set the tone in this regard. We needed something simple but tangible to remind us of our vision and values. Therefore, we solicited proposals from consulting firms that specialized in that sort of thing, and the fact that the quotes for the project ranged from eighty to four hundred thousand dollars was a shock. Considering that I have a Scottish heritage, it was obvious that we would not go that route. So instead, we decided to offer a two hundred dollar prize to the employee who came up with the slogan which truly represented our purpose and mission. The vice president who suggested this approach said that she believed this would work even more effectively than outside consultants because "we know ourselves better anyway."

A formal contest was held and the prize of two hundred dollars (that was worth a bit more back in those days) encouraged more than two hundred entries. Interestingly, but not surprisingly, the winning entry was submitted by one of our nurses. I say that because I believe nurses are the backbone of the organization; they work "where the rubber meets the road" in hospitals. And what a wonderful credo the winning slogan was. *"PROFESSIONALLY WE SERVE, PERSONALLY WE CARE."* A four hundred thousand dollar consulting engagement could not have brought us a more appropriate one.

For the next twenty five years, our employees were constantly reminded by this short statement that serving and caring were our main products. By the way, there are a couple of interesting sidelights to this story. First, the nurse who won the prize came by to see me the next week and said that she wanted to donate the two hundred dollars to the building program we had underway. I knew that she certainly could have used the money herself, but instead she gave it back.

Second, because I was so moved by the slogan as well as her attitude, I asked Pat to share her thoughts and ideas with me about this special statement she had created. She said, "To professionally serve is to give our skill and abilities to our patients; to personally care is to give ourselves to them." We both had tears in our eyes that day when she left my office, and forever embedded in my heart was a principle which changed my life. The only calling higher than serving is caring. That was our vision!

> **The only calling higher than serving is caring.**

Defining the vision is the beginning; maintaining focus on it for the long haul is the desired end. The following lessons were the result of the effort to sustain our emphasis on serving and caring.

LOVE ALL YOUR BROTHERS

I am one of those folks who needs to be constantly reminded, so I think perhaps everyone else needs reminding, too. Here is one of the reminders about caring service that I passed along to my fellow workers via the hospital newsletter one month:

Several weeks ago, I learned unexpectedly that my brother had been in a serious automobile accident. He was conscious when he arrived in our emergency room, but was very irritable and combative before they rushed him to surgery. He must have suffered a head injury, I thought. "Did you treat him well? He's my brother," I anxiously asked the E.R. secretary.

I called surgery to make sure that the anesthesiologist and surgeon knew that he was my brother. "He's special. Do your best," I told the recovery room nurse. "Take good care of him. He's my brother."

About the time he was to go to the intensive care unit, I was called into an important committee meeting. As the session dragged on, all I could think about was my brother upstairs in critical condition. I stepped out for a moment and called the unit. "Give him the best nursing care available. He's my brother," I frantically requested. They kept him in isolation overnight because there was risk of infection. I asked the evening supervisor to make certain he was comfortable and well-cared for. "He's my brother," I told her. I hardly slept that night. I prayed that he would recover completely.

Even though I have worked in health care for many years now, sometimes it seems impersonal. I often get bogged down in day-to-day activities and I forget that we are treating people, real people. I sometimes even forget that our true purpose is to professionally serve and personally care. But, when my brother came into the hospital, I immediately regained my perspective and our sense of purpose was very clear to me.

As I walked in the door the next morning, I was told that my brother was out of danger and had been transferred to a regular nursing unit. I could visit him for the first time. Before going up, I called every department that had served him to thank them for taking such good care of my brother. Interestingly, most had not realized that he was the brother of the CEO of the organization because his last name was different from mine. They were just doing the usual good job of serving and caring, as they always do.

It seems to me that this is what a hospital is all about—special people giving special care to patients who are very special to folks. In other words, to serve our brothers and sisters.

Because I am the only boy born into the Brown family, I guess I was just thinking that because all men are my brothers, I need to love and serve them all.

> **Because all men are my brothers, I need to love and serve them all.**

"Whoever loves God must love his brother."
—1 John 4:21

SURE WE CAN CRY

I learned a lesson one day that went counter to my training. I had been taught that I was not supposed to get too emotionally involved with patients and that "real men" don't cry. However, I cried one day at work. I closed the door to my office and actually cried. This emotional outburst was the result of three visits with patients. I knew these folks personally and each of them was considered part of our hospital family because of our volunteer program. All three had cancer.

The first was a volunteer who had been fighting this disease for more than fifteen years. She had been an inspiration to me and had helped numerous other patients suffering from the same illness. She had tears in her eyes as we talked about her involvement at the hospital. She didn't know what the immediate future held, but I could sense a peace about her during my visit.

The second was a volunteer who grew some of the most beautiful roses I had ever seen. Many of our events were adorned with her flowers. During our conversation she told me about how her doctor had broken the news to her family about her disease. She shared with me the fact that she was not concerned about herself but instead she was worried about "her boys" because they were so worried about her. I noticed sadness in her face as she told me all this, but there was also a certain peace about her.

Then I stopped by to see the son of one of our newer volunteers. He was a college student and an outstanding young man whose courage had touched the hearts of all those around him. For you see, he had lost a leg to cancer earlier and was again in a battle to arrest the disease. We talked for a long time, and during the course of the conversation, he mentioned several of our employees by name who had given him such loving care. He let his emotions show, but despite this, he too, had a special peace about him.

I share these three experiences with you because I learned something significant that day. I had always been told that doctors, nurses and other hospital people are supposed to refrain from becoming emotionally involved with patients because it makes their jobs too hard. We are not supposed to cry. However, after thinking about this a great deal, it seems to me that there is nothing wrong with crying. It would be hard to really care for folks if you couldn't cry with them.

> **It would be hard to really care for folks if you couldn't cry with them.**

I did not know that day what the future held for these three special people, nor do I know what it holds for any of us. However, I do know after three visits which I had a hard time making; I felt I had been blessed. I went to give, but I received. On second thought, I do know what the ultimate future holds. I hope that you do, too!

(Note: Within a year, I was asked to sing at the funerals of all three of those with whom I visited that day. I was at peace because I knew that they were at peace.)

"I have compassion for these people..."
—Mark 8:21

GIVERS OR TAKERS

The idea of being service-oriented or a servant, if you will, goes against our natural "grain." Instead, we would rather be served. To a degree there is a battle going on within each of us between humility and egotism, and which side wins is ultimately decided individually. Follow the logic of this lesson which began with a common word game.

Once I was involved in an intense game of Trivial Pursuit. It was at that crucial point where a right answer would have given my team the last slice of pie. Victory was in sight. Here was my question: "What is the most used word in the English language?" I debated whether it was "the" or "a" and then settled on "the." To my amazement, neither was correct. The most used word in our language is "I."

For some reason, I began thinking about the implications of "I" being our most popular word, and to be honest, I came up with some mixed feelings about this. From one standpoint, does this imply that I am a selfish egotist because I primarily dwell on the things which benefit me personally? Am I constantly seeking those things which satisfy my own desires and appetites?

Or does this extraordinary use of the word "I" infer that even though I might be a bit self-centered, I do have the ability to exercise control over my own attitudes, goals and objectives. Am I trying to raise myself above my own selfish interests? Am I seeking a higher purpose in my life and as a result will this be a better place because I passed this way?

While pondering this philosophically, I soon realized the excessive use of "I" is neither good nor bad in itself. Instead, the thing that determines whether this popular pronoun has a positive or negative connotation is the verb which most often follows it. In other words, is "I" most often followed by a selfish verb (I have...I want...I take...), or is "I" used more in a selfless sense (I give...I serve...I care...)? From all of this I have concluded that we tend to be either givers or takers in our life's journey and the way we use "I" in our daily communications generally conveys which we really are.

> **From all of this I have concluded that we tend to be either givers or takers in our life's journey and the way we use "I" in our daily communications generally conveys which we really are.**

After reviewing what I just wrote in this lesson, I counted the times I used the word "I" (or its derivative; i.e., me, my). According to my count "I" was used 49 times. Now I know why "I" is our most used word.

"Do nothing out of selfish ambition or vain conceit, but in humility consider others better than yourselves."
—Philippians 2:3

WE CAN AT LEAST CARE

Our slogan, *Professionally We Serve Care, Personally We Care*, taught me that there is a difference between serving and caring. There were times, because of circumstances beyond my control, when I could not "serve" but I do not remember a single time that I could not "care."

It never ceased to amaze me how little things often made the difference in regard to an individual's, as well as an organization's, success or failure. I have found, for example, just to express concern can often compensate for one's inability to solve a problem.

Years ago, I rented a trailer to carry my daughter's "things" back to college for her senior year. As usual, I was in a hurry when I picked it up on Friday afternoon so that we could load for our trip on Saturday. After the trailer was connected to my car, the lights would not come on, so we decided to hook up another one, which also failed to work. It became obvious that the problem was not the trailer, but the connector which came with the car. Incidentally, I had never pulled a trailer nor used the light connector with this car before. After about an hour of frustration, I told the manager of the rental company that I would take the trailer as is and go down the street and have the connection checked out by the car dealer where I bought the car just a few months earlier.

I pulled the trailer into the service department to ask for assistance fifteen minutes before closing time. My hope was to exchange the malfunctioning connector and be on my way to load up before dark. The initial response to my plea for help was, "We can't do anything 'til Monday."

"All I need is a new connector," I explained.

"We don't have them in stock."

"What can I do? The part that came with the car doesn't work!"

"Who sold you the car? Go ask him."

By now, my frustration had turned to anger, so I went into the showroom to see the salesman who was so accommodating when I bought the car. He showed sincere concern for my dilemma and escorted me back out to the service department. It was obvious that he had no authority with them because their response to him was similar to that which I had received earlier.

As we walked back to the car and trailer, he said, "I don't know anything about the electrical system, but I'll take a look at it anyway." He went over and checked the connector and jiggled the wires and said, "Try it." To my amazement, the brake lights worked, both blinkers worked and the tail light also worked perfectly. Evidently, all that was needed was a mere adjustment to the connection. That salesman was my hero, but the service department was a villain in my eyes. And in the way of human nature, the bad experience stuck in my mind, leaving me with a negative feeling about the whole thing. What if the service man had just taken two seconds to show concern and jiggled the wires himself? Even if his attempts had failed, I would have felt that he cared about my predicament, and my impression of the situation would have been entirely different.

I learned a lot from this experience. Even though you cannot always serve, you can at least care. It seems to me that when we really care for each other, "the lights go on."

> **Even though you cannot always serve,
> you can at least care.**

"This service that you perform is not only supplying the needs of God's people but is also overflowing in many expressions of thanks to God."
————*2 Corinthians 9:12*

THE VALUE OF BEING ORDINARY

For some unknown reason, I tend to be attracted to people who do not "put on airs" or exhibit lofty social status. Interestingly, such folks are often found in hospitals, among all the ranks including doctors, nurses, technologists, therapists, housekeepers, assistants, analysts, accountants, managers and in every other group. Sometimes I wonder why I like these "plain ordinary folks" so much.

One day, I discovered a clue to my feelings in this regard. I had been working in the yard and came in for a glass of ice water. The cabinet shelf next to our refrigerator houses three kinds of glasses: first, we have some expensive ones with our initial on them; then we have some nice Coca Cola glasses; and finally, on the bottom shelf we have a group of unmatched jelly glasses. These are the ones we collected years ago when jelly and jam were sold in jars which, when emptied, could be used for beverage glasses. You guessed it, on that day as I typically do; I selected one of the jelly glasses for my ice water. It's also interesting to note that the jelly glasses are nearly impossible to break and are almost always the first ones to reach the dish washer between washings. In other words, these ordinary glasses are my favorites.

I am attracted to plain folks for the same reason I am partial to jelly glasses. I just seem to be comfortable with them. They don't intimidate me because they are not pretentious or overly fancy. They are practical, not fragile, and are always accessible. But probably their most important attribute is their faithfulness. They have been with me through thick and thin and particularly during my early times. Be they my plain ordinary friends and acquaintances or my jelly glasses, I just have a great affection for them.

It seems to me that many with whom I have worked in health care are a lot like those jelly glasses—sturdy, dependable and able to get the job done without a lot of fuss. Both deal with the most basic human needs without ever losing their charm, and the older they get, the more valuable they are! From one jelly glass to another, you ordinary folks are extraordinary to an ordinary person like me. I have come to realize that most patients are also just ordinary folks who are attracted to caregivers who have those same attributes.

> **From one jelly glass to another, you ordinary folks are extraordinary to an ordinary person like me.**

(A little side note: at a recent antique fair, I saw a jelly glass just like one of mine priced at $20.00, the same price we paid for the entire set of six Coca Cola glasses. The glass that cost me nothing initially now is my most valuable one.)

"...nor will I ever betray my faithfulness."
—Psalm 89:33

APPRECIATING COMPLAINTS

Despite our best efforts, we do not always do it right. We fail to meet the expectations of our customers. What then? Here is one thing we can do.

One day a gentleman came by my office to complain about the service his wife was receiving. After we had discussed his concerns and resolved the immediate problem, I said, "I appreciate your complaining to me." He responded in surprise by asking, "Do you mean you like to hear complaints?" I went on to explain that though I didn't particularly *like* them, I did *appreciate* them.

Here was my logic. It was my observation that most people complained only when there was a legitimate reason. Even if the service was excellent, yet perceived to be poor, complaints still resulted. When we heard about it, we did our best to fix it. Therefore, if folks were going to complain about our organization, I had rather that they came directly to me or to some responsible members of our team. Unfortunately, some of those we served who had problems while in our care tended to complain, gripe or criticize us among their friends and acquaintances without going through the proper channels. I had a hard time appreciating those kinds of complaints which usually got back to us second hand.

I once had an experience that brought this principle home to me personally. While traveling with my family, we stopped at my children's favorite restaurant, a quaint little place called McDonald's. While I ordered, my wife and daughters went to the restroom. When we sat down to eat, my wife, Snookie, commented on the terrible condition of the women's restroom. We carried on a conversation right in the middle of the eating area about that restroom. (By the way, this was very atypical of our previous experiences at McDonald's.) Then she said, "I think I should tell the manager," and proceeded to do so. To our surprise, he graciously thanked her and within thirty seconds a worker was dispatched to clean up the mess. I was even more impressed when both the manager and the employee thanked us again as we left. Evidently they appreciated our complaint.

It seems to me that human nature often causes us to be defensive when we receive complaints about our work. However, we can develop a servant spirit that makes us genuinely appreciative of complaints. I appreciated those who complained to me, for whether they realized it or not, they helped us improve. I was equally thankful when I did not get more than I could handle in one day.

> **We can develop a servant spirit that makes us genuinely appreciative of complaints.**

"Better is open rebuke than hidden love."
—Proverbs 27:5

(And When I Did Not Appreciate Complaints)

I received a call from a man whose mother had been in our hospital. He started the conversation in a very negative, accusing manner, and it was obvious that I was about to get a complaint. He stated that our billing system had a defect, and his mother had received an incorrect statement. He wanted it straightened out now. If I did not take care of this *post-haste*, he indicated that he would go directly to the hospital board.

I listened for a few minutes. Then my human defensive, egotistical reaction to such pressure took over. In short, I told him what I thought of his tactics and approach. Then he reacted to my reaction and so on. We had a real scene on the telephone which ended abruptly with a "click."

Shortly afterwards, either due to a sense of guilt or maybe just curiosity, I went around to the billing department and looked into his complaint. I wanted to prove what an idiot this guy was. With the personnel in that department, I discovered that there was a defect in the data processing program which would result in erroneous statements being sent to a limited number of patients in a certain category. I never dreamed we could be wrong.

The problem was corrected with some minor adjustments in the program. My angry caller would not receive another incorrect bill. I could forget it. But I couldn't. My conscience began to poke me. Although the problem had been solved, I had made an enemy for our hospital because of the way I had handled this situation.

Finally I called the man back, apologized and explained the whole thing to him—exactly what we had found and how we had corrected it. It was amazing how he reacted this time. I think we made a friend then.

It seems to me that we certainly can make life hard for ourselves at times. It is interesting to observe how the right attitude can often alleviate the greatest of problems, while the wrong attitude can turn the smallest problem into a large one. I learned another lesson that day.

> **It is interesting to observe how the right attitude can often alleviate the greatest of problems, while the wrong attitude can turn the smallest problem into a large one.**

"He must make full restitution for his wrong..."
—Numbers 5:7

SERVE WITH GRACE

There is more than one way to serve. This helped me!

In 1979 Alan Alda (the actor who played Dr. Hawkeye Pierce on the television series M.A.S.H.) was asked to address the graduating class of the Columbia University College of Physicians and Surgeons.

Some of Mr. Alda's observations have application to all who work in the health care field. He stated, "...Be skilled, be learned, be aware of the dignity of your calling...but please don't ever lose sight of your own simple humanity in the process...I only ask one thing of you: Possess your skills, but don't be possessed by them...You have a monopoly on medical care. Please be careful not to abuse this power that you have over the rest of us...I show you my body, but I bring you my person. Finally...there is one thing you can learn about the body that only a non-doctor would tell you, and I hope you'll always remember this: The head bone is connected to the heart bone, and don't let them come apart."[3] It seems to me that this make-believe doctor had great insight from which we can all profit. To serve is noble; to serve with grace is divine.

> **To serve is noble; to serve with grace is divine.**

"Each one should use whatever gift he has received to serve others, faithfully administering God's grace in its various forms."
—1 Peter 4:10

WHEN THINGS GET PERSONAL, AN OBLIGATION BECOMES A PRIVILEGE

Serving is a mind thing; caring is a heart thing. This was never clearer to me than when I shed my blood for something special.

The Red Cross bloodmobile came, and I went by to donate my blood. Usually around nine o'clock in the morning the initial crowd had cleared, but in this instance the line was backed up the corridor all the way to the cafeteria.

I had a meeting at ten, so I knew that I wouldn't have time to be processed. I returned after lunch but found a similar situation and then again during the middle of the afternoon, but the line was still very long. Finally, at 6:30 that evening they finished taking my blood.

I was the next to last of 282 who gave that day. This was a one-day record for us that might never be broken. Normally, 100 units were considered excellent.

What made this particular blood drive different from all the others? A few weeks earlier, the son of one of our best nurses was injured in a near-fatal accident at a construction site. As a consequence, David lost a leg, had multiple operations and would require extensive therapy for several months. In the course of his treatment, he had received around 95 units of blood. Thank goodness he had come a long way and would continue to improve.

The Red Cross had publicized the fact that it was short of blood this time of year; but more significant in this case, word had spread that one of our hospital family needed blood. In addition to our folks, people from David's church, Dobbins Air Force Base, where his father worked, and Lockheed, the employer of one of his aunts, contributed greatly to the success of this drive.

More important than the record number of donors, many individuals gave blood for the first time. Several had to overcome fear of the needle. I even saw several doctors donating their blood.

That particular blood drive by all accounts was special. It seems to me that it was special to most of us who participated because it was personal. You see when things get personal with us, our spirits rise and what before was considered an obligation becomes a privilege.

> **When things get personal with us, our spirits rise and what before was considered an obligation becomes a privilege.**

I signed my name to David's get well card while I was drinking three cups of fruit juice and eating more than my share of peanut butter cookies. Then I left immediately to attend the monthly Utilization Review Committee meeting, and I was back in the real world of hospital business. But for that few minutes while my blood was being taken, I thought to myself, "This is what we are really here for!" PROFESSIONALLY WE SERVE, PERSONALLY WE CARE!

"Entirely on their own, they urgently pleaded with us for the privilege of sharing in this service..."
—2 Corinthians 8:4

THE REST OF THE STORY

I began this chapter by telling how our organization's slogan originated. Now, fast forward approximately twenty five years. Even though I had moved from Kennestone Hospital after several mergers and consolidations into a corporate office miles away, I was invited back for a party celebrating my retirement. Several hundred folks were present including some of the "old timers" but most were newcomers. In some responsive remarks following their expressions of kindness toward me, I told the story of the slogan. When I got to the point of reminding them what it said, without any prompting all joined me emphatically in unison:

"PROFESSIONALLY WE SERVE, PERSONALLY WE CARE."

What a great departure gift. *"Professionally We Serve* means giving our skills and abilities; *Personally We Care* means giving ourselves!" They got it!!

57

PROFESSIONALLY WE SERVE, PERSONALLY WE CARE

(Note: For marketing and public relations purposes this slogan was neither the first nor last one for the organization, but from my view point it had the greatest impact.)

"Jesus said, 'Take care of my sheep'."
—John 21:16

PROFESSIONALLY WE SERVE, PERSONALLY WE CARE

"Where there is no vision, the people perish..."
—Proverbs 29:18 KJV

Questions for Further Study and Discussion

1. Does your organization have a slogan? Is it widely known both inside and outside the organization? If you were asked to create a personal slogan for yourself, what would it be?

2. Do you give better service to those you know personally? How do you treat those whom you do not know well?

3. Is there a danger in caring too much for those you serve? Should you maintain your distance?

4. Is the word "I" your most used word? Can you recognize those among you who are givers? Can you recognize the takers?

5. Can you serve without caring? Can you care without serving?

6. Are you attracted to the "plain and ordinary" folks? Do you consider yourself "plain and ordinary?"

7. What is the difference between liking and appreciating complaints? Do you avoid listening to complaints?

8. How is grace related to service?

9. Have you ever experienced having an obligation become a privilege? Explain.

10. Do you professionally serve and personally care in your job?

FACING PROBLEMS, CHALLENGES
AND OPPORTUNITIES

"Consider it a joy...when you face trials of many kinds..."
—*James 1:2*

Inherent in leadership is the need to address problems. However, the issue in regard to these regrettable happenings is not how many or even how big the problems are, but instead how effectively they are handled.

Pessimists tend to enlarge problems, while optimists sometimes underestimate their significance. However, both mindsets at least acknowledge the existence of these potential obstacles to personal and organizational fulfillment. Some define problems as challenges, but if approached correctly they can also be opportunities. One thing is certain, personal, professional and spiritual growth would not occur without problems/challenges or opportunities.

The story about the shoe salesmen conveys an interesting contrast in perspectives concerning opportunities. The first salesman was sent to a remote region of a third-world country to evaluate shoe sales opportunities. After two weeks, he wrote, "I am coming home. No one wears shoes here."

A second opinion was suggested, so another salesman was dispatched. In only two days a message was received back at the home office: "Tremendous opportunity for our products. No one wears shoes here!"

How we view our circumstances can also be the cause of a problem or the source of an opportunity. Often, the question is whether our circumstances are on top of us, weighing us down, or whether we are on top of our circumstances, viewing from above the possibilities for resolution and fulfillment. What we are talking about here is the *"altitude of our attitude."*

I have discovered that problems are like weeds. When facing them, we usually just mow them down like we do our grass but do not eradicate them. Therefore, they tend to keep coming back. Like a weed, we must destroy the problem's root before it truly can be solved.

This all sounds good, but how can you be positive in the midst of overwhelming problems, or in biblical terms how can you be joyful when you face trials of many kinds? I can honestly say that I do not have all the answers but I have learned a few lessons in regard to problem-solving. First, it really helps to have help; second, it really helps to have help from someone who has the answers; third, it really helps to have help from the One who has the answers and then follow his directions; and finally, it really helps to have help from the One who has the answers, follow his directions and learn from the experience.

> **First, it really helps to have help; second, it really helps to have help from someone who has the answers; third, it really helps to have help from the One who has the answers and then follow his directions; and finally, it really helps to have help from the One who has the answers, follow his directions and learn from the experience.**

If I just remember this, my relationship with God changes from being the *choice of last resort* to having him be my *source of first response.*

The following are some of the problems that I have encountered that posed genuine challenges but became real opportunities and some of the lessons learned as a result.

DIFFICULT CUSTOMERS

What if most of your customers were difficult? How would you handle it? Most business endeavors have a few problem customers, but in my business most of ours seemed to be difficult. I came to this conclusion many years ago when my only son was a teenager.

When Jeff was 16 years old, he was one of the greatest joys of my life. He was not full grown yet, but he could already beat me on the tennis court (most of the time) and could slam dunk a basketball on our backyard goal, which we had lowered a foot from regulation height. And he made decent grades, too.

But if you have ever had a teenage boy, you know it isn't all good. At times he could be rude, self-centered and even downright ornery. Although I loved him more than most everything in life, I often found myself not liking him very much because of his behavior and manner. However, from conferences on raising teenagers, conversations with other parents and my own memory of being a teenage boy, I had concluded that he was as normal as apple pie. During the period when a boy is passing from childhood through adolescence into manhood, he is just not very easy to get along with. He can drive you up the wall and many times you really have to work at liking him.

While I was dealing with this, I noticed that there was another group of individuals who were also not very likeable at times. I found that many patients were, like my son, hard to get along with. They were hurting, they were often mad, they were very demanding, they were preoccupied with their own problems, and in general they just were not in a good frame of mind. All of these and other traits made them poor candidates for "most likable" among our acquaintances.

I wondered, as health care professionals charged with the responsibility of serving these sometimes unlikable people, how would we deal with our tendency to strike back, respond negatively or be apathetic about their needs? It seemed to me that our situation here was similar to my relationship with my son. If that be the case, we needed to look at it from the same perspective.

We needed to realize that people who were usually quite amiable could become self-centered, demanding and even obnoxious in an alien setting like a hospital. Most were going through a dramatic and often critical event in their lives. To hospital workers this could be a source of frustration or it could be the opportunity for great satisfaction, depending on how we responded. Anyone can love the likable, but only special people can love the unlikable. I discovered that it was the nature of hospital folks to love the latter, perhaps in the same way that a father loves teenage sons.

> **Anyone can love the likable, but only special people can love the unlikable.**

Jeff is now happily married with two children and has a highly successful consulting career; he is a strong Christian, active in his church. This is a little surprising to me, not because he was not capable, but because I didn't do away with him before he was seventeen.

"...as a father the son he delights in."
—Proverbs 3:12

PREPARING FOR CHANGE

In today's world, a major problem is managing change. In the health care business in which I worked, as in life in general, we could be assured of only one thing – change was coming. Because of this, I spent much time thinking about preparing for change.

I learned a principle about readying oneself for change one day while bird watching. The principle was this: "Don't get too comfortable today, because tomorrow you'll have to leave the security of your nest."

We had just moved into our new house on the lake. While in the backyard, we spotted a nest at the top of a tall maple tree which, with the help of binoculars, we learned housed two baby red-shouldered hawks.

Over the next few weeks, we watched the mother hawk bring bugs, frogs, snakes and lizards for the youngsters. As the baby hawks grew, we noticed they were starting to sit on the side of the nest and then venture further and further out on the adjacent branches. They began spending less time in the nest and more time out in the tree.

At first, I thought that the main reason the young left the nest was because they grew too large to fit into it. However, in researching the habits of hawks, I learned that the parent birds include briers and thorny vines in their nest-building materials. The intent of this unusual practice is to make the nest very uncomfortable for the young birds as they grow larger and heavier. As a result, they willingly leave the nest to experience the next phase of their life—learning to fly. If you ever watch a hawk ride the wind currents in lazy loops, you just know that bird is experiencing the joy of flying. Yet to gain that pleasure, it first had to endure discomfort.

It seems to me that we humans may go through some of the same phases of life as a hawk. I have often desired to continuously lounge around in my comfortable "nest," only to feel a prick from a thorny situation. It is these experiences which often cause me to move on to something more important and productive. Maybe the lesson here is that we should not look at our painful and unpleasant experiences in a negative manner, but instead view them as an inducement to step out and attempt bigger and better things.

> **We should not look at our painful and unpleasant experiences in a negative manner, but instead view them as an inducement to step out and attempt bigger and better things.**

A few months later, I was awakened by the triumphant cry of a large bird. When I looked out my window, I saw a fully grown red-shouldered hawk in the sky with a small snake in its beak for breakfast. I had a feeling that the young hawk enjoyed the meal it caught for itself even more than the ones its mother brought to the nest.

The next spring the hawks came again to remind me of this important lesson in life. It is often a painful experience on the launching pad that impels one to soar to great heights. But perhaps we then will be ready for the changes that are sure to occur.

"...the birds of the air have nests, but the Son of Man has no place to lay his head."
—Matthew 8:20

DIFFERENT PERSPECTIVES

Over the years, I have learned that two or more people can look at the very same situation and see something totally different. This, probably as much as any other factor, leads to breakdowns in communication and potential conflicts within an organization.

This point became obvious to me years ago during a visit from some of my relatives. It related to a collection of paintings, drawings and carvings of old men that hung on the wall of our den. I was very proud of this collection because it had taken years to accumulate. I assumed that everyone would appreciate this unusual display of art as much as I did.

While riding up for a long weekend with us, my nephew Jonathan, who was five years old at the time, asked his mother if he was going to have to sleep on the sofa in the den this time. When Betsy, my sister, asked him why it mattered where he slept, he replied, "There are pictures of weird men hanging on the wall in the den. I think one of them might even be a killer!" It was interesting to think that something that was art in my eyes struck terror in the mind of a young child.

From time to time I could see disagreements among members of our team. I heard arguments among professionals. I observed confusion and frustration among doctors, employees, patients and families. We tried and tried to communicate, yet we often did not seem to be on the same page or to understand where others were coming from. Certainly much of this was a natural result of being in a complex, dynamic organization, but could we do anything to improve communication and understanding among those with whom we interacted?

This was a very real problem, but it seemed to me that we could try. First, we could listen to others, and I mean really listen with openness and respect. Second, we could recognize that others may be coming from a different direction; therefore, they might have a different perspective than ours. If we really did listen to others, we might even learn something and find a common ground of understanding.

> **If we really did listen to others, we might even learn something and find a common ground of understanding.**

After giving this some thought myself, I truly tried to take it to heart personally. I remembered someone saying one time that God gave us two ears and one mouth so we should listen at least twice as much as we talk.

After listening to Jonathan, I found that there was one picture in particular that frightened him. I examined it very closely and, you know, the old man did look a bit like a killer! The next time Jonathan and his family came to visit I took it down. Then, I decided to take it down permanently just in case others might feel as Jonathan did.

> *"Everyone should be quick to listen, slow to speak and slow to become angry..."*
> —*James 1:19*

FIGHTING LOW MORALE

We had just relocated into a brand new facility. I was stopped in the hallway and asked this question: "Is it normal to have low morale in a department that has just moved into beautiful new quarters?" The inference was that at least one department was having a morale problem.

According to Mr. Webster, morale is an attitude. Therefore, poor morale is a poor attitude.

After giving this question a little thought, I remember that I had personally suffered from poor morale after the completion of certain major programs in which I had been involved. Maybe it's just human nature to have a let-down in spirit after reaching a goal toward which one has strived for so long. There are bound to be start-up glitches. When the systems that were designed to solve all of our problems do not function perfectly at first, our attitude can easily sour. Things just aren't what they used to be. We have to re-think how to do the things we did automatically before. It takes some shake-down time before we feel comfortable again.

So it is probably perfectly normal for morale to droop a bit in beautiful new quarters. However, the real issue is not the fact that this can and does occur; it is instead what we are going to do about it. Here are some suggestions that I developed for myself for these and other occasions to counter low morale.

First, *step back* and get a true perspective of the situation. Is it as bad as it seems? Or are we perhaps overreacting?

Second, *step up* and raise yourself above some of the seemingly important yet often petty issues which are causing problems in attitude.

Third, *step down*, humble yourself and realize that you don't know all the answers to all the problems. You are going to have to depend on others to help you.

And finally, *step forward* and realize that though much has been accomplished, there is a great deal yet to do. Know that while low morale might be the problem, you can be part of the solution.

Step back
Step up
Step down
Step forward

Morale is an attitude but it is also of a spiritual nature.

"A man's spirit sustains him... but a crushed spirit who can bear?"
—Proverbs 18:14

IT'S NOT MY JOB

What makes an organization a great one rather than just a good one? Let's take a hospital for example. Do you think of programs like organ transplants, cancer research or high tech services when you think of a great hospital? Certainly major programs like those are often found in great hospitals. But in my opinion, there is another way to measure greatness, particularly when viewed through the eyes of the patient.

Surveys which we conducted periodically revealed that patients we served did not usually mention the breadth of institutional services or even the outcome of their illnesses. Instead, when asked to evaluate their experience in the hospital, they mainly recalled the attitudes and responsiveness of the people who served them. A helpful, friendly, caring attitude stayed in their minds; and unfortunately, the reverse was also true in some cases.

This topic came up once during lunch with one of our most respected doctors. This was a practicing physician who I knew loved and cared about his hospital; I valued his opinion. He expressed concern over what he called the "little things" which detracted from the image and reputation of the organization. He proudly stated that the "big things," the life and death functions, were handled beautifully. A trauma case or critically ill patient could receive no better care anywhere, he bragged. But missing the little things we should routinely catch could make us fall short of our potential. He made an observation that stuck with me. He said, "Perhaps we have too many areas where everybody is responsible, so nobody is responsible."

This brought to mind an incident that occurred in one of the first hospitals in which I worked. A patient knocked over a cup of water, spilling it on the floor beside her bed. Anxious to avoid slipping when she got out of bed, she asked the nurse's aide if she would mop it up. The patient had no way of knowing that hospital policy stated that small spills were the responsibility of Nursing, while large spills were to be cleaned up by Housekeeping. The aide, after looking at the puddle, decided that it was a large one, so she called the Housekeeping Department. Upon observation, the housekeeper saw the spill as a small one.

The two employees began arguing over the size of the spill there at the patient's bedside. The nurse's aide stated, "It's not my responsibility, because it's a large puddle." And the housekeeper said, "No, it's not mine, because it's too small." The patient listened for a minute, and then exasperated over what she was hearing, took her water pitcher and poured the contents on the floor. "Is it big enough now for you to decide?" she asked.

From all of this I would make two points. First, we often are judged more on the "little things" rather than the big things that occur in our jobs. And second, we all must be responsive to the needs of those we serve. The words, "It's not my job" should not be in the vocabulary of anyone who serves.

> **"It's not my job" should not be in the vocabulary of anyone who serves.**

"But they all alike began to make excuses."
—Luke 14:18

QUALITY VERSUS COST

In most business decisions, a tension exists between quality and cost. There is often the belief that improving the quality of a product can reach the point that it is no longer affordable and will not sell. In other instances, making a product so cheaply can diminish interest in it by customers because its quality is, or is perceived to be, inferior. I reconciled this dilemma in my own mind while on a business trip.

While in Canada some years ago attending the joint American/Canadian Hospital Association convention, I purchased an addition to my collection which I had been accumulating over many years. As mentioned earlier, I collected paintings, drawings, etchings, carvings and sculptures of "old men." In this type of art, one can see and feel real character and wear on the face of an old sea captain, or the concentration and determination of two old gentlemen taking one another on in a game of checkers, or peaceful anticipation being experienced by an old fisherman on the river bank with a cane pole, or painful courage on the face of an old soldier.

In Montreal, I bought a wood carving of a rugged old bald-headed man from the North Country. Though it was relatively small, the details on the face, clothes and shoes were outstanding. I was thrilled to add this little statue to my modest collection. An interesting thing about this piece of art was an inscription on its tag. It said, *"l'amertume d'une qualite' medicore demeure longtemps après qu' on a oublie le bas prix."* Interpreted, this means, "The bitterness of poor quality lingers long after the sweetness of low price is forgotten."

> **"The bitterness of poor quality lingers long after the sweetness of low price is forgotten."**

I couldn't help but relate that little saying to the hospital business in which I worked. While hospitals ought to be dedicated to maintaining the lowest possible prices, it should never be forgotten that the patient's well-being must come first. In such facilities, quality is the most important product. Hospitals owe it to those who trust them with their lives. When the names of our hospitals were mentioned, I always wanted those names to be synonymous with outstanding quality service.

"A good name is more desirable than great riches; to be esteemed is better than silver or gold."
—Proverbs 22:1

THE NEED FOR A PERSONAL TOUCH

It seems that we are becoming more and more dependent on computers in every aspect of our lives. From a business standpoint this is good because it allows us to be more efficient and productive. On the other hand, we can easily slip into the habit of blaming the computer for all our shortcomings and thus become quite impersonal in dealing with the public.

In his book, *Megatrends*, John Nesbit pointed out the trend toward high tech and also cited the need for high touch in the services we render.[4] In our case it was especially important that we remembered how much patients needed the human touch.

Actually, we all long for that human touch, and nearly everyone has a "man versus machine" story to tell. Here is mine which occurred some years ago when the computer age was just beginning.

On a weekend my wife sent me to buy some ice cream and to cash a check so she would have some spending money. She gave me her Honest Face Card (a computerized ID card used back then when cashing personal checks) which I had never seen before.

I picked up the ice cream and then went to the cashier who instructed me to have my check approved by a machine with my Honest Face Card. So I got in a long line to wait my turn. I followed the instructions given me by the machine—inserting the card, entering data, etc. The trouble began when it asked me for my "secret code." Since I had never heard of a secret code, I asked the gentleman behind me, "What's the secret code?" He indignantly replied, "I'm certainly not going to give you MY secret code!"

After he realized my dilemma, he helped me retrieve my card, which was a feat in itself. Card in hand, I went to the pay phone (this was before I had a cell phone) to call my wife, only to discover that I didn't have a cent. Fortunately, the fellow who had helped me in the line was kind enough to give me a quarter. He probably was anxious to get this incompetent individual out of the store.

When my wife answered the phone, I demanded to know the secret code. She started laughing so hard that I almost couldn't understand what she was saying. Personally, I didn't see anything funny about it.

I wrote down the code, got back in line and went through the whole process again. Just as I was at last completing the chore, I read, unfortunately too late, the final instructions: "Place your check face down." The machine did its thing, quickly stamping its approval on my check and regurgitating my card. The approval stamp was printed right across the front of my last and only check. Embarrassed, humiliated and defeated, I walked slowly back to the cashier who kindly said, "Don't worry; other folks have done the same thing. I can fix it."

I trudged into the house and handed my wife her money and the ice cream that I had purchased almost an hour earlier. With a twinkle in her eye, she thanked me for the half gallon milkshake.

I learned from this and many subsequent experiences that a machine can never provide the personal touch which folks so desperately need in a hospital and in fact everywhere. Unfortunately, if anything, the trend toward high tech and "low" touch has intensified. Even though I am probably more sociable than most, much of my daily interaction with others is through answering machines, e-mail, faxes and blackberries. I hear far more human voices from my radio, television and CD player than from real live people. I truly believe that this is one of our greatest problems; we have lost the personal touch. As never before, we need to be together, to help and encourage one another, to share with and to care for each other and to provide the personal touch.

> **As never before, we need to be together, to help and encourage one another, to share with and to care for each other and to provide the personal touch.**

"...and all who touched him were healed."
—Matthew 14:36

THE WAR WITH WORRY

I used to worry a lot. I spent half my time worrying about those things that I didn't have, and then I worried the other half away about losing the things I did have. I worried some about my problems, but I tended to worry much more about my blessings.

Then one day I came to the realization that worry was not only negatively influencing my own effectiveness, but in time would probably be detrimental to my health and well-being. It was easy to decide to stop worrying, but I quickly learned that it is probably harder to actually stop worrying than it is to stop smoking. (Even though I have never smoked, I can sympathize with those who attempt to quit "cold turkey" because of the similarities between these two addictions.)

Worry is a terribly destructive force in our lives. I once heard someone say that worry is to the body and mind what rust is to a machine. Worry is a bad habit that most of us have, and we need to address it as any other negative attitude which we possess. I imagine that there are "worry cessation clinics" in existence, but most of us would be too vain to seek them out. Therefore, it may be more practical to analyze our own worries and expose them for what they are.

In my case, most of my worries concern things I can do little or nothing about. I generally find that if I could do something, then I wouldn't be worrying. So I'm left primarily with those situations over which I have no control. What can be done about these? In analyzing this dilemma, I discovered that when I turn these things over to someone who can do something about them, I no longer need to worry. I have been doing this for years now, and as a result, worry is no longer one of my major bad habits.

I once heard an interesting chronicle on worry. It goes something like this:

When you think about it there are only two things in life to worry about: whether you're sick or well.

If you're well, then you don't have anything to worry about. But if you're sick, then you have two more things to worry about: whether you're going to get well or die.

If you get well, then you don't have anything to worry about. If you die, then you have two more things to worry about: whether you'll go to heaven or hell.

If you go to heaven, you don't have anything to worry about. But if you go to hell, then you've really got something to worry about. And for a long time. [5]

Oh! If we could just take a pill or stick on a patch to remove our addiction to worry! There is a pill called *trust*, and there is a patch called *faith* that can really help. As a health care professional, I should know!

> **There is a pill called *trust*, and there is a patch called *faith* that can really help.**

"Who of you by worrying can add a single hour to his life?"
—Matthew 6:27

DEALING WITH THE DOLDRUMS

After a long, hard day, have you ever wondered, "Did I do anything worthwhile today?" I once thought that was an inherent problem only with jobs like mine, but in talking with others, I came to realize that many felt the same way.

Meetings were my albatross. There were days when I attended as many as twelve meetings. I had started before breakfast and ended around midnight on a few occasions. I can recall when asked by my children, "Dad, what does an administrator do?" answering, "Attend meetings all day!" Even following good meetings, I often asked, "What have we accomplished?"

Paperwork was a chore that many of our skilled professionals cited as their thorn. A computer operator commented one day, "Why are we creating so much data that no one seems to use?" I talked with a disgruntled painter, who had repaired and painted a hallway twice, only to have it scratched and marred again by a cart or a stretcher. A laundry worker exclaimed, "It's raining linen; we will never finish!" Even my wife expressed frustration after cleaning, shopping, cooking and taxiing all day because the next day was going to be more of the same. The implication in these and many other examples is, "Why am I doing all this?"

All this and more made me wonder if our society in general and our organization in particular were bogged down in meaningless activities which had little or no redeeming value. However, in the midst of all this wondering, I looked around and saw what was being accomplished. Meetings often fostered good communication and teamwork, which resulted in progress. Needed plans and programs were initiated. Paperwork and computer data documented the quality of our services and provided a permanent reference in good decision-making. An attractive environment fostered by freshly painted walls and clean linen was not only comforting to our patients, but also deterred the spread of disease and infection. And maybe most importantly, my wife's sometimes routine, monotonous, thankless duties helped make a home for her, our children and me, which was a haven of blessings and a place of peace.

I guess the point in all this is that at work as well as in the rest of life, many of our activities seem meaningless, but when viewed from the broader perspective, most of them do fulfill some overall purpose.

Nan Freeman, a pharmacist and special person in our organization, once shared a little story with me about her children when they were small that shed some light on this subject. Her sons complained while raking leaves, "Mom, why do we have to do this? More leaves are just going to fall." Nan answered, "Yes, but the next time you will be raking different leaves."

It seems to me that if we can remember that life is an endless process of raking different leaves, then it might not seem quite as tedious or unfulfilling. I remember this little lesson very vividly every autumn when the leaves are so beautiful in my backyard before they fall. It makes the raking and raking and raking again all worthwhile.

> **If we can remember that life is an endless process of raking different leaves, then it might not seem quite as tedious or unfulfilling.**

"And the leaves of the tree are for healing…"
—Revelation 22:2

DISPELLING DISSATISFACTION

Do you like your job? Let me share a story that might make you think twice about this question.

Jim had been in his present position for several years, but felt things were not just right. He knew that there was something better out there for him. He enjoyed his work, but it was not exactly what he wanted. He had even looked around a bit to see what other opportunities existed in the marketplace. However, nothing exciting had materialized. So one day he decided to resign his position in order to search full-time for that ideal job which had eluded him so far in his career.

The first few weeks of unemployment Jim used to prepare his resume and career objectives and to rest up for this major effort. He started reviewing ads in newspapers and professional journals concerning available jobs. He contacted friends and past associates for leads. Even though he wanted to stay in the same general area, he soon found himself looking into opportunities in other cities. But nothing seemed to be right. After two months, Jim, in frustration, decided he needed to use a professional employment agency to assist him in his quest. Certainly these experts could find just the right position for him. But two more months flew by and the right match between man and job did not develop.

By now, Jim had exhausted most of his savings, and frustration was turning into depression. He felt that he was well-prepared and had been an excellent employee in the past, so why couldn't he find that special, ideal job somewhere out in the big world, waiting just for him?

Then one day a friend called Jim's attention to a block employment advertisement which appeared in the classified section of the large Sunday edition of the newspaper. It was a blind ad, so he didn't know the company's name or exact location. But the description of the position seemed perfect. He had the exact qualifications required, and the duties and responsibilities were just what he was looking for. In his mind, he had finally found the perfect job and he was going all out to get it.

Jim immediately sent his resume in to the newspaper. He alerted the individuals he had listed as references. He even had his best suit cleaned and his shoes polished in anticipation of an interview.

In a few days Jim was surprised to get a call from his old boss, who said, "Jim, we would like for you to come back to work. We haven't been able to replace you with anyone nearly as capable, so your old job is open again."

Jim didn't know how to respond; he felt torn. Should he go back, or should he continue to pursue that "perfect" job for which he had applied? To Jim's astonishment, the dilemma was resolved in a few seconds when his boss continued, "It surely was good to hear from you, but you should have just contacted me directly. You didn't need to send your resume through the newspaper."

The grass always appears greener on the other side. We often feel the opportunities are greater, the pay is better, the work is easier, the stress is less and the job is ideal "over there." However, when talking with some of the folks over there, we sometimes learn that they have the same view of us "over here."

We all get dissatisfied from time to time in our situations; such is the nature of humans. However, I ultimately came to the conclusion that there is a plan that includes where I am supposed to be. I felt that when I was bagging groceries, when I went off to college, when I moved from place to place and ultimately became the CEO of a large organization. I still sense that even in retirement and as I pen these thoughts.

> **I ultimately came to the conclusion that there is a plan that includes where I am supposed to be.**

"Commit to the Lord whatever you do, and your plans will succeed."
—Proverbs 16:4

HEALING EMOTIONAL WOUNDS

Working in an organizational setting with others is not always easy. At times, it can be much like a battlefield with all the ramifications of war. You try your best to avoid injury or being wounded. Someone once told me that running a hospital would be easy if we didn't have to put up with all these patients, doctors and employees.

I can remember suffering from a number of "wounds." Generally, they were not physical but were of a mental or emotional nature. Some resulted from personal conflicts; several were caused by disappointments and a few I would classify as intentional "stabs in the back." If you have ever experienced afflictions such as these, you know how much your feelings can be hurt.

From these and other instances, I have come to the conclusion that emotional wounds are much like physical ones and should be treated similarly. Let me give you an example. When I was a kid, I remember stepping on a nail, and though my sock and tennis shoe were bloody, I just kept on playing the rest of the afternoon. Later, the wound became infected and fairly drastic treatment was needed before healing occurred.

Now that I'm older and wiser, I realize that certain precautions should be taken after a wound such as that. First, cleanliness should be maintained around the site; second, an antiseptic agent and dressing should be applied; third, time should be allowed for the healing process; and finally, functional use should be restored as soon as possible before atrophy takes hold.

It seems to me that emotional wounds would respond to the same kind of treatment. *Cleaning the wound site* could mean determining to keep your mind on a higher plane and refusing to give in to your first, emotional and often illogical responses to the hurt. Also, forgiveness washes away bitterness and the urge to get even.

Applying an antiseptic agent and dressing to your emotional wounds involves getting the proper perspective on the cause. For me, this means prayer (talking it over with the Lord), and peer support (sharing my thoughts with a trusted confidant). These two applications provide spiritual and emotional "medicine" that often takes the sting out of life's battlefield encounters.

The next step is applying *tincture of time*. The old saying goes, "Time heals all wounds." (I have heard it turned around to say: "Time wounds all heels.") It is amazing how, with the simple passage of time, wounds lose their ability to hurt us, but this requires patience.

Finally, we come to *rehabilitation*, also an important part of emotional healing. I don't want to let negative experiences turn me into a bitter, cynical person, so I have to make a conscious decision to risk trusting others again.

Interestingly, the "nails" that inflict emotional wounds are generally other people. Yet, we must always remember that nails, properly used, hold our houses together. Likewise, our relationships with others are what hold our organization and even our society together. I hope that this lesson hit the nail on the head for you.

> **The "nails" that inflict emotional wounds are generally other people. Yet, we must always remember that nails, properly used, hold our houses together.**

"He…healed those who needed healing."
—Luke 9:11

PROBLEMS ARE NECESSARY

Problems! We all seem to have them. They are sort of like the weather, because everyone talks about problems, but nobody seems to do very much about them. Problems exist in all aspects of our lives. We often wonder how much easier our lives would be if only some of our problems would go away. Those of us who claim to be optimists like to call our problems opportunities, but still they tend to upset and frustrate us.

The downside to including a section in this book devoted to problems is that it can go on forever. There is no end to the possibilities of identifying and addressing organizational problems. The attempt in this chapter has been mainly to create a mindset that places these in a different light, for without problems and challenges there would be little need for most organizations and their leadership to even exist. So let me sum all this up with some final observations about these things we call problems.

• Problems are the learning lab of life. Dealing with them makes us grow. Some of the wisest people I know have worked their way through a host of problems.

• Many problems cannot be permanently solved. As mentioned earlier, problems are like weeds: they can be cut back, but until their roots are destroyed, they can return.

• To me, my problem is more important than your problem. To you, your problem is more important than my problem. We often fail to listen to or help others with their problems because we are preoccupied with our own. Expressions of understanding, concern and empathy for another's position might help us all to better solve, or at least cope with, our problems.

• Personal problems tend to create organizational problems, and I'm certain the reverse is also true. If only we could keep from worrying about our personal problems while we are on the job, and leave work problems behind when we go home.

• Problems don't cause us to fail. However, failure to handle problems spoils success.

• Problem-solving can be fun if approached from a positive standpoint. An example of this is the handing of complaints. My office tended to be the complaint department, so I started accepting complaints as a personal challenge. My objective on any complaint was to correct the problem and make a friend out of the complainer. I didn't always succeed, but it was a whole lot easier to face a problem in this manner.

If I lived my life without problems, I would neither grow nor mature as an individual. Our greatest lessons may be learned from our worst problems, provided we lick them instead of allowing them to whip us.

> **Our greatest lessons may be learned from our worst problems, provided we lick them instead of allowing them to whip us.**

So I will end as I began this chapter.

"Consider it pure joy...whenever you face trials of many kinds..."
—*James 1:2*

FACING PROBLEMS, CHALLENGES AND OPPORTUNITIES

"Consider it a joy...when you face trials of many kinds..."
—James 1:2

Questions for Further Study and Discussion

1.   How do you turn a problem into an opportunity? Is it wise to be a constant optimist?

2.   Are some customers so difficult that they are not worth serving? Can you love the unlikable?

3.   Have you ever felt thorns in your nest? What did you do about them?

4.   How hard is it to see someone else's point of view? What if that someone's perspective is just the opposite of yours?

5.   When your morale is low, what do you do to change it? Have you ever helped someone else boast their morale? How did you do it?

6.   Have you ever said to a customer, "It's not my job?" Are the "little things" missed more often than the "big things" in your organization?

7.   Is the quality or cost of your services given the most emphasis? When you buy something, which is the most important?

8.   Have the "high tech" aspects of your organization had any adverse affect on the "high touch" component of its services? If so, how can you improve the situation?

9.   Are your "worry habits" distracting from your effectiveness? Can you turn over your worries to someone else and not then take them back?

10. What is your albatross (greatest burden) in your work? Does "raking different leaves" have any meaning to you?

11. How would you rate your satisfaction level in your work? Is there an ideal job out there for you?

12. What kind of emotional wounds have you experienced? How have you dealt with them?

13. Does the word "problem" have a negative connotation to you? If so, what can you do to change your perception of problems?

EXPERIENCING HUMOR AND OTHER EXPRESSIONS OF JOY

"And Sarah said, 'God hath made me to laugh, so that all who hear me will laugh with me'."
—*Genesis 21:6*

"Laugh and the world laughs with you; cry and you cry alone." Even though I don't totally subscribe to that philosophy, aren't we all drawn to a person with infectious laughter? We had a man in our organization whose laugh made all around him laugh, too, though they often didn't know why. I have known others whose demeanor was habitually so glum and gloomy that I almost felt depressed in their presence. It's not hard to figure out with which one you would rather be.

Even the most serious events often have a humorous side. For instance, when Sarah and Abraham learned that they were to have their first child at ages 90 and 100, the Bible tells us that "Abraham fell upon his face and laughed" and Sarah laughed, too. Can't you just see those two old folks rolling with laughter at the wonderful absurdity of it all? In fact, they named their son Isaac, which means "laughter."

Laughter has been called the best medicine because of its physical, emotional and spiritual value. A good laugh oxygenates the blood and stimulates the brain to produce serotonin, bringing us a rush of energy and elation. I love to be around people who are happy and see the humor in life.

Humor is abundant. The human condition is full of absurdity, as Sarah and Abraham could attest, and it's liberating to acknowledge that we're all prone to unexpected happenings, silly mistakes, goofy encounters and ridiculous situations.

I believe that among the most blessed are people who can laugh at themselves. Once we take a small step back from a problem and see the humor in it, we have already taken a giant step forward toward mastering it. This is particularly important to those who are in leadership roles. I have found that many leaders seemingly take themselves too seriously, and therefore, miss the joy which can come from laughing at themselves. The hospital business in which I worked is a serious business; however, proper applications of humor, fun, candor, adventure and other expressions of joy also have their places in this organizational setting. I learned many important and significant lessons from situations which, at the time or later, were down right hilarious.

An abundance of joy should be found in every person's life including his/her job. This chapter may not have great philosophical value, but if it makes you laugh and you learn a few lessons from these true experiences, it will be worth it. So lighten up and join me!

> **An abundance of joy should be found in every person's life including his/her job.**

A SENSE OF HUMOR

Mahatma Gandhi once said, "If I had no sense of humor, I would long ago have committed suicide."[6] In an attempt to demonstrate that I didn't take myself too seriously, I asked a carnival artist to do a caricature of me. I planned to use it on my monthly newsletter column. Some to whom I showed it initially said, "It doesn't look like you." Others commented (probably more honestly), "Unfortunately, it looks just like you." My rebuttal to all of them was, "What do you expect for two dollars?"

A caricature by definition is a ludicrous distortion of characteristics; its purpose is to humorously depict one's distinguishing features. Will Roger put humor in perspective for me when he stated, "Everything is funny as long as it is happening to somebody else."[7] I used the caricature only a couple of times on my column heading because of all the harassment I received from my friends.

What does this have to do with organizations and how they are run? Some may say nothing. However, it seems to me that even in the most serious and sober activities, there is a place for humor. I have seen it relieve tension, restore relationships, express affection and even communicate a caring attitude. "Good humor isn't a trait of character; it is an art which requires practice,"[8] according to David Seabury. I think we and our organizations would be far better off if we would practice this art more often. It surely helped me.

> I think we and our organizations would be far better off if we would practice the art of good humor more often.

"...and your face is lovely."
—*Song of Solomon 2:14*

THE FUN IN FAILURE

Have you ever been demoralized by a mistake or failure, and because of it, you withdrew into your shell and hesitated to move on to bigger and better things? I surely had the tendency to do just that. Dwelling on my shortcomings often made me a far less potent manager and leader. I have thought many times, if only I could have kept going and not let those errors affect me, how much more effective I would have been.

An experience which I had when I was about eight years old reminded me of the principle of "keeping on keeping on." All the children in my family were required to take piano lessons for at least a year. At the time, I considered such activities as sissy, but now regret that my instrumental career was so short. The entire year tested my mother's patience and fortitude because ball games were far more exciting to me than piano practicing.

My year's effort culminated with the annual recital held at the school auditorium, which featured students of several of the local piano teachers. I was in the last group to perform and my selection was to be "The Wigwam Song," from the John Thompson beginner book. I was already insecure due to my lack of talent and commitment, and we were required to play "by heart." I became totally intimidated when I learned that two students under different teachers had also chosen "The Wigwam Song" for their renditions.

My teacher had told us to stay calm and to keep going even if we made a mistake and that stuck in my mind. This was also probably the first time I ever seriously prayed. In short, I was petrified.

I remember looking out at the audience, making my bow and mounting the piano stool. Then the worst of all happenings occurred. After playing the first couple of lines, I totally forgot how to end the piece. I remembered another song that I had learned, so I began playing it. By sheer accident, I managed to merge the two melodies. Still unable to find an ending, I abruptly finished my presentation with some sort of modern-sounding discordant "bang."

As I walked off the stage, I noticed the reluctant applause of my teacher and empathetic relief on the face of my mom. My only thought was that I did what my teacher said. I stayed calm and kept going even though I made a mistake.

Today, I still believe that principle is crucial to one's success, as well as peace of mind. I have lost count of my miscues and, thank goodness, I do not dwell on them much anymore. I have learned to just stay calm and keep going. Despite my failure at the key board, my love for music was born as the result of this experience.

I have learned to just stay calm and keep going.

This little story had a humorous ending. As we ate cookies after that recital many years ago, I remember hearing one of the local "sophisticated" ladies say to my mom in all seriousness, "I could not believe how well Bernie played. He performed such an advanced version of the 'The Wigwam Song'."

"…calmness can lay great errors to rest."
—*Ecclesiastes 10:4*

LAUGHS ON OURSELVES

Humor and funny incidents seem to happen unexpectedly and at the most interesting times. I remember a very hectic, even chaotic time when we were struggling to form a large, multi-hospital alliance during a period when the entire health care industry was experiencing major upheaval. In short, there was very little to laugh about.

However, during times of constant stress and strain, it is always refreshing and uplifting when something truly funny happens. Let me share such a personal experience. It occurred on the night of the annual Teem Lecture at Kennestone Hospital. This symposium honored the late Dr. Martin Van Buren Teem, Sr. and served as the premier educational event for our medical staffs each year. Dr. Louis Sullivan, former Secretary of Health and Human Services, was our speaker, so we had a record crowd on hand.

During dinner in the large cafeteria, I left the head table and went back to the service area to get some nonfat frozen yogurt for dessert (I was trying to stay on my low fat/low cholesterol diet). Near the yogurt machine, I spotted three individuals who had wandered into the cafeteria by mistake. They planned to get a cup of yogurt too, but were embarrassed when they realized that they had entered an ongoing meeting. They reminded me a bit of a squirrel in the middle of a road with a speeding car coming. They didn't know which way to go. In an attempt to be helpful and alleviate their anxiety, I walked over and asked them if I could help, explaining that the cafeteria was closed to the public because of the meeting. "We are so sorry!" they kept saying. I did not have my name tag on, so they knew neither who I was nor where I worked. But in an effort to put them at ease since they were already in the midst of all the activity, I offered to give each of them a cup of yogurt. To this they replied, "No, that's alright." But I was determined to be customer-friendly. So I said again, "Please, let me get you some yogurt." But they responded emphatically, "No, we can't take it. We don't want to get you in trouble! Thanks anyway." And they left in a hurry but with a smile. I chuckled all the way back to my table.

Soon afterwards I was listening intently to Dr. Sullivan's presentation on health care reform. He covered heady issues such as the need for cultural changes, freedom of choice, biomedical research, tort reform, the role of government and individual responsibility.

As my brain was swirling with the dynamic, complex subject of the lecture, I thought back to my encounter by the yogurt machine and I had to laugh again. All my sense of self-importance as the institution's CEO being in the forefront of these momentous changes was punctured by those good folks who didn't know or care who I was. Yet, they were very sensitive and thoughtful because they didn't want to get me in trouble.

I was reminded again that as long as health care involved human beings, we would always find some reason to laugh now and then. And some of the best laughs are the ones we have on ourselves. My work was really fun at times.

> **Some of the best laughs are the ones we have on ourselves.**

"Our mouths were filled with laughter…"
—*Psalm 126:2*

TIME MARCHES ON

Funny happenings often convey important lessons. The story I'm about to tell you is going to date me! Some of you will nod you heads in recognition, and others will wonder what in the world I'm talking about. It depends entirely on how old you are. When I graduated from high school, my parents gave me a watch, a gold one. It was the best thing I'd ever owned, and I was proud of it because it came at a special time in my life with love from my mom and dad. I wore it for the next forty years with one exception. I got a more modern watch for fishing, one that was water-proof. But at all other times, I wore my graduation watch.

One day a young staff member saw me winding it, and inquired, "What are you doing?"

"Why, I'm winding my watch," I replied.

"Winding a watch; what's that?" she asked.

Talk about a generation gap! My young friend had never heard of watches that needed winding because she had grown up in a quartz, battery-operated time-keeping world. I, on the other hand, grew up in a day when watches and clocks were wound by hand and there was some ritual to it. You tried to wind them at the same time every day; not over wind which could break the winding stem, yet not let them run completely down.

I realized that my graduation watch belonged in the "old world" of timekeeping. All watches did in those days was tell the time. They didn't beep or chime or give you messages or tell you the day, month and the year. They were relatively expensive and you tried to keep them running and in good repair for as long as possible.

My fishing watch, however, was "new world" all the way. It took a tiny battery, never needed winding, didn't mind getting dunked, and was so inexpensive that when it no longer ran, it would be cheaper to replace it than to fix it.

Those of us who have one foot in the "old world" and the other in the "new world" can at times be easily confused and funny things can happen. One day when I was still at the hospital, I drove to the parking deck and reached out to swipe my badge through the gate scanner. To my embarrassment, I realized that I was wearing two watches on the same arm. I certainly knew what time it was that day. But some might argue that I didn't know which end was up!

From this funny experience, I recognized some similarities between timepieces and health care delivery. This lesson has been mentioned earlier but cannot be over emphasized. We could call the "old world" of health care—*high touch*. Like my graduation watch, it required hands-on attention. High touch health care meant just that. Although there was ever-increasing technology, patient care was more directly delivered by the skilled hands of professionals. The "new world" could be characterized as *high tech*. Anyone who has recently visited an Intensive Care Unit can testify to the bewildering maze of cords, tubes and monitors that link each patient to sophisticated machines and equipment. Those help save lives but they can not convey compassion. While we all value the latest and best diagnostic and therapeutic tools, we also long for the touch that only another human being can give.

All this reminds me that both high touch and high tech are necessary as never before. We must give our communities the best of both worlds. Our mission will always be to deliver the highest quality professional service with a human, caring touch. All organizations should have this same purpose. I believe that the *time* will always be right for this and that is why perhaps it was okay to wear two watches including one which had to be wound.

> **This reminds me that both high touch and high tech are necessary as never before.**

"…the old has gone, the new has come!"
—*2 Corinthians 5:17*

THE LURE OF THE KILLER BEE

Even during enjoyable times of recreation and respite, lessons can be learned.

Here is one of those quick but lasting ones that have "stuck" with me. Justin Burgstiner, one of my very best friends, tells the story about an experience he and I had when we were teenagers. Or course, he embellishes and exaggerates this yarn a bit, but here is my version.

While fishing one day, I found a "fly" (small artificial lure) on an overhanging limb at the edge of the pond. Evidently, another fisherman had lost it earlier. The fly was in good shape, so I stuck it on my shirt collar for safekeeping.

As we finished fishing at the end of the day and were paddling the boat toward shore, Justin noticed a "bug" on my collar. He shouted, "There's a bee on your shirt!" I could see its wings through the corner of my eye, so I started slapping the "bee." Of course, this was the fly that I had rescued from the limb. Each time I hit it, the hook stuck in my shoulder and felt like a bee sting. My last hope to rid myself of this killer bee was to go overboard, which I proceeded to do. It was only after I was soaked to the gills that I remembered placing the fly on my collar.

Here are a few lessons I learned from that experience. First, we tend to have lapses of memory; second, artificial replicas often look like the real thing; and third, we sometimes react drastically without having all the facts. Certainly these are natural human traits, but because they can be harmful at times, we need to develop means to counteract such tendencies wherever possible.

You know, life might be awfully boring and mundane if we had the capacity to remember everything, to see everything clearly and to act appropriately in every case—in other words, to be perfect. It seems to me that a more realistic approach is to recognize our human frailties and take appropriate steps to overcome our weaknesses. To consider ourselves perfect is the height of human vanity; to be effective despite our imperfections is the epitome of human achievement. This is the lesson that has stuck with me.

> **To consider ourselves perfect is the height of human vanity; to be effective despite our imperfections is the epitome of human achievement.**

"Don't let anyone deceive you in any way..."
—2 Thessalonians 2:3

TO SHOOT A MOCKING BIRD

This is probably my favorite true story. John Bowling, the current CEO of the Hamilton Medical Center in Dalton, Georgia, worked in our organization at one time early in his career. John is an extremely likeable and able guy, and he and his family are dear friends of ours. Although he is a man of many talents, I discovered an area in which he was completely inexperienced when I took him on a dove shoot.

As we were riding out to a small pond on the edge of a corn field, John leaned over to me and whispered, "What does a dove look like when it's flying?" I just could not believe that a boy from southern Mississippi had never been on a dove shoot before. However, this was particularly important to John because we were going to be hunting with a bunch of local "good old boys" who had been bird hunters all their lives. To keep him from being embarrassed, I told him that when the first dove flew over, I would loudly call out his name as a cue.

This was a good idea, but it just didn't work out the way we planned. I was using a new shotgun for the first time that day and because I was unfamiliar with its operation, a shell became jammed as I was loading it. I needed to borrow a pocketknife to dislodge it, so I yelled, "John…" John immediately rose from behind a few corn stalks, gun pointed toward the sky. A mockingbird had the misfortune of leisurely flying over us at the time. Three shots rang out in succession and the bird fell dead in the middle of the small pond. John felt elated until he heard the rest of my question: "…can I borrow your knife?"

That incident reminded me of a management philosophy that I heard described as "fire, ready, aim." Sometimes we are so eager to get off shots that we do not look carefully enough at the target. I learned some practical lessons from this little incident. First, be careful when you select hunting partners—remember this person will be armed and in your vicinity. Second, be cautious when you give someone instructions; make sure that what you say is what you mean. Then do what you say. Third, make certain your equipment is in good working order and that you know how to use it. And, finally, when you're flying high, watch where you're going.

John has allowed me to tell my version of this story probably a hundred times (he tells it a different way). Despite our kidding each other unmercifully for over forty years, we have remained friends; I consider him one of my best! We have hunted, fished, and played golf, and our families have even vacationed together many times since this incident. We have fought organizational battles together; we have advised each other; and we have worshiped and prayed together. All of these and many other things are what good friends do. However, probably the one thing that has strengthened our friendship most of all is the fact that we laugh a lot together.

> **Probably the one thing that has strengthened our friendship most of all is the fact that we laugh a lot together.**

"Like a bird that strays…"
—*Proverbs 27:8*

A PINK BUBBLEGUM SLUGGO

I always felt that those of us who worked in health care needed to practice what we preach. In addition to promoting healthy lifestyles, we should also live them. For example, we should eat a well-balanced diet, exercise faithfully and have regular check-ups. But just as important, we need to engage in stress-release activities. One of my favorite of these is a good laugh every day.

I was either fortunate or unfortunate—I can't always decide which—to work with a group of people who really believed in laughter. Sometimes the joke was on me. (You might have thought that CEOs were exempt from ridicule?) Let me share one.

Every year I used to take the office staff to lunch in observance of National Secretary's Day. Several years ago when the day came, it happened that I was the only man in the office. "No problem," the women assured me, and everyone crowded into my car. We had an enjoyable lunch and as we were leaving the restaurant, I remarked that I was going fishing during the coming weekend and wanted to stop at Wal-Mart to buy a new plastic worm lure I'd heard about called a Pink Bubblegum Sluggo. "But I'll stop on my way home tonight," I said.

"Look, there's a Wal-Mart right there," one of my companions observed. "Why don't you just run in now?"

It will only take a minute, I thought, and I turned into the store parking lot.

I figured my friends would wait in the car, but no, they all piled out and followed me into the store. Then I presumed they would browse through the women's department while I went to sporting goods, but no, they followed right along behind me. I walked as fast as I could, thinking I could lose them in their high heels, but amazingly they kept right up.

Once we got to sporting goods, they fanned out and began searching for the lure, and they did not shop quietly.

"Oh, look, here's a cute pink one," one called to the others.

"Hey, how about this one. It's a nice shade of pink."

"Does it have to be pink? This lavender one is darling."

I could feel my face getting hot as I tried to put more distance between myself and my helpers. But no matter how hard I tried to pretend I didn't know them, they stuck to me like glue. My humiliation was complete when a big burly guy in a "gimme" cap looked me up and down and said in a falsetto voice, "Ooooh, I gotta get me some of them cute little pink ones, too."

I couldn't get out of that store fast enough—with no fishing lure, by the way—but right behind me I could hear the click-click-click of those high heels, along with a lot of muffled giggling. I didn't trust myself to speak, but they knew I was mad and there was very little said on the way back to the office.

The next day there was a paper bag on my desk and when I opened it I found a package of Pink Bubblegum Sluggos. If laughter really is the best medicine, it seemed to me that my friends were in the best of health that day. In retrospect, I was honored that the office staff felt comfortable enough to include me in their "good laugh" that day. I must have been leading from the bottom.

> **I was honored that the office staff felt comfortable enough to include me in their "good laugh" that day.**

"A cheerful heart is good medicine..."
—*Proverbs 17:22*

A PAIN IN THE NECK

I feel that one of the main reasons patients are often so upset, frustrated and distraught when they come to a hospital is because their world has been turned upside down without warning. An experience some years ago led me to this conclusion and thank goodness everything turned out fine; it even got funny after awhile.

I was fishing on Labor Day on a lake where my close friend Bucky Smith lives. This was the last outing I would have with my oldest daughter Jenny, who would soon leave for college. We had a successful catch and were having a great time.

My last cast was with a red Rapalar (this lure looks like a small gold fish) and, unfortunately, it got hung in a weeping willow tree on the edge of the bank. I couldn't pull the lure loose so I just kept jerking it. Finally, it dislodged and flew right back, hitting me in the neck under my ear. It didn't hurt much, but I realized that one of the hooks had penetrated the skin. When Jenny tried to assist me in removing it, she managed to stick another one of the hooks in my neck. After surveying the situation, we decided that we had better go home immediately and ask for Mom's help. While riding home, I felt very conspicuous with a bright red lure hanging down from my neck. As we passed cars, I was careful to turn my head.

When we walked into the house, my wife immediately turned pale and demanded that I go to the emergency room. I remember saying to myself, "I'm not going to embarrass myself by walking into our emergency room with that thing hanging down like a bright earring." I only agreed to go after wire cutters had severed the lure from the hooks, and I had called the emergency room and told them that I was slipping in the back door. Fortunately, it took the doctor only about five minutes to remove the hooks.

My point in sharing this experience with you obviously is not to brag on my fishing skills, but to point out how our lives can be changed in a split second. I had gone from the height of personal enjoyment to the depths of a traumatic experience in one stray tug on a fishing rod.

When I think of the changes in people's lives caused by an automobile crash, the discharge of a gun, severe headaches, chest pain or the discovery of a spot on an x-ray or scan, I can really understand why patients can be so upset and distraught. It seems to me that health care providers have a tremendous responsibility and opportunity to serve at a time when not only professional, but also personal care is badly needed. We never know when we may join the ranks of patients. Isn't it funny how an experience can be funny later when it was anything but funny at the time?

> **Isn't it funny how an experience can be funny later when it was anything but funny at the time?**

(A side note: About eight years after this incident, we bought a house across from Bucky and Susan Smith and have lived on that same lake ever since.)

"...haven't you any fish?"
—John 21:5

EVERYONE NEEDS A MASCOT

Sometimes I take myself too seriously. I can remember back during one of those times, I had an unusual visitor to my office. This person walked right by my secretary, entered my office unannounced, looked me in the eye, patted my shoulder, hugged my neck and left. Not a single word was spoken during this visit, but in just a few minutes my attitude was transformed. After that first encounter I saw that same individual often, and every time my spirits were lifted.

My visitor was "Kenneroo," the kangaroo mascot at that time for Kennestone Hospital. It started me thinking how much fun mascots are, and that maybe we should all have our own mascots to help us rally when we are down. For instance, physicians could be represented by the serpent because it is a part of the *caduceus*, and because it is wily and wise. Nurses might choose the dove to exemplify their gentleness, tranquility and a caring attitude. Technologists and therapists might have a beaver because they tend to be diligent and precise. Service and support personnel could choose the horse, denoting hard workers. My secretary said clerical workers would be bees or clams because "we are always busy and must clam up at times." Volunteers may be swans because of their graceful contributions to our organizations.

I was stumped for awhile about what mascot should represent the chief executive officer, but I finally settled on the opossum (or as we call it in the South, the 'possum). Let me share my rationale for this selection. A 'possum is ugly in appearance; most CEOs aren't much to look at, either. A 'possum instinctively lies down and plays dead when in danger. This is a technique many CEOs have learned to use for self-preservation. 'Possums have more teeth than any other mammal and can be vicious fighters when cornered. Need I expound on that? Because of intrusions into their natural habitat, many 'possums have been forced to live in densely populated areas. They often try unsuccessfully to cross busy highways; therefore, the attrition rate is high. At the end of a typical day, many CEOs also feel like they've been run over by a big truck. 'Possums often hang by their tales; CEOs, too, are often left dangling. 'Possums have the ability to maintain complete immobility for long periods of time, thus conserving their strength while thinking deeply. CEOs, too, can strike this pose (some call it sleeping in meetings).

But 'possums serve a purpose. They are scavengers, cleaning up after others and doing some of nature's dirty work. The CEO's role in an organization contains surprising similarities. By and large, it is not a glamorous job either.

Finally, and most importantly, 'possums are great survivors. They have adapted and flourished longer than many of earth's other inhabitants. Some theorize that they are one of the few surviving prehistoric animals.

CEOs face constant change and must possess adaptive skills or they will surely perish.

I used to read a comic strip called *"Pogo,"* which was about a 'possum and his friends from the Okefenokee Swamp. Interestingly, my Mom and Dad grew up in Waycross, Georgia, next to that swamp. Maybe that's why I sometimes feel like a swamp rat and why I can identify so well with my mascot—the 'possum.

This was an interesting and fun exercise. It provided me a means to objectively look at myself and my job without hurting my own feelings. You may want to try it yourself sometimes.

> **It provided me a means to objectively look at myself and my job without hurting my own feelings.**

"But ask the animals, and they will teach you..."
—*Job 12:7*

TRYING CAN BE TRYING

Everyone has a mother-in-law story. I end this chapter with mine. Annette is a professional artist—wonderfully talented but more importantly, my favorite mother-in-law! She not only paints but also taught art for many years. She firmly believes that everyone has some type of artistic talent which can be released if he or she will just try. She even convinced me to try when she gave me a set of acrylic paints and brushes. The issue then became what my first subject would be.

In my travels, I tried to visit hospitals around the country. My favorite was Pennsylvania Hospital which was built in 1751 and is the oldest in the United States. I had a photograph of the main entrance of this historical institution, so I decided this was what I would paint. If it turned out well, I planned to display it in my office.

Because of my insecurities in this first attempt as an artist, I did not want to invest in a real canvas. Instead, I discovered that the back of some wall paper we had on hand resembled a canvas and would serve the purpose.

On my first effort, I learned how to mix the paints for desired colors and to make it all appear proportionate, but the final result wasn't too great. Thus, since I had to start over, my decision to use the wall paper proved prudent. I cut another piece for my second attempt and to my surprise, this one was quite good. In fact it was so good, I planned to have it framed for my office.

When I took it to the framing store, a young lady helped me select just the right mat and frame to match my other office wall hangings. I was feeling very proud of myself, knowing I listened to my mother-in-law and had released my artistic talent for others to enjoy. But, as I was leaving the store, a young man from back in the production area rushed out with one last question about my desire for the framing. In all innocence he asked, "Mr. Brown, which side do you want to show?" What a put down! What a blow to my ego! Yet, in his defense, the front side of the wall paper was rather pretty.

Despite this extreme damage to my confidence, I choose to hang it in my office anyway. About a year later, my office was moved to another location and the interior decorator banished my masterpiece to the work room. It even decorated the small office bathroom for a while before disappearing entirely. When I retired and was moving my stuff out, I found it tucked behind a file cabinet. It now is hidden in our attic to be "discovered" when I am gone.

I was asked to try; I tried; I did it; I wasn't good; I was actually humiliated. But, this experience has really made a good story and a lot of folks laugh. From this, I have learned that to try is not a failure; failure to try is!

> **I have learned that to try is not a failure;**
> **failure to try is!**

"...a time to weep and a time to laugh..."
—Ecclesiastes 3:4

EXPERIENCING HUMOR AND OTHER EXPRESSIONS OF JOY

"And Sarah said, 'God hath made me laugh, so that all who hear me will laugh with me'."
—Genesis 21:6

Questions for Further Study and Discussion

1. Do you have fun at work? Do you know any funny stories that have taught you some serious lessons?

2. Do you have a good sense of humor? Do others think that you do? Do you ever try to raise the spirits of others by making them laugh?

3. Have you ever really failed at something, which you now consider humorous? How did you feel at the time it occurred? Why can you now laugh about it?

4. Have you ever been intensely focused on something and a funny incident happens that gives you some comic relief? Have you ever laughed at yourself in front of others? Give an example.

5. Have you ever done something really stupid which made your day more enjoyable? Did you tell anyone about it?

6. When the joke is on you, does it make you mad? Can you tell a humorous experience about others and not make them feel uncomfortable?

7. Do you have friends, with whom you just enjoy laughing? Have you ever laughed so hard that you almost lost your breath?

8. Are you the kind of person whom others throughout your organization enjoy being with? Is fun, laugher and humor part of your organization's culture?

9. If you were to select a mascot for your organization, what would it be? If you had to select a personal mascot, what would it be?

10. Have any of your serious endeavors turned out to be hilarious? Do you enjoy sharing these experiences with others?

11. What is the difference between happiness and joy? Have you experienced true happiness? Have you experienced pure joy?

DISCOVERING TRUE SUCCESS

"Let another praise you, and not your own mouth; someone else,
and not your own lips."
—*Proverbs 27:2*

As I approached the end of my professional career, I remember looking back with a sense of pride and accomplishment. In my early years as a leader, I greatly coveted personal recognition, and even though this desire had subsided a bit, I still liked to hear my name called when the trophies were passed out.

I played tennis in college and many years afterwards, which instilled an intense competitive nature in me. I was a chief executive officer of a major institution at age 31. Professional, civic and personal titles and honors have all come my way over the years. Downstairs in my home, I once had a hallway full of plaques, certificates, trophies, cups, clocks and pictures noting those different achievements. In short, you might call me an egotist even though I would like to give the opposite impression. To some extent, I guess my human nature will always drive me in that direction.

However, a couple of years before my retirement, I gained a slightly different perspective of meaningful achievement. A young man who had worked several years in our organization from student status to a vice president level was leaving for a better position in a large institution out of state. At his going-away party he said a lot of nice things about his relationship with me and how much it had meant to him. Afterwards, one of my board members came up to me and said, "You should really feel great about the impact you have had on so many young people you have worked with. You will look back on these relationships as one of your greatest accomplishments."

As I drove back to my office, I reflected on the many young administrative residents and aspiring executives with whom I had worked for over 30 years. In my office, I kept a file in my desk of special notes and letters that I received. I pulled out the folder and started reading some of them. Several dozen were from professional colleagues with whom I had worked. All expressed appreciation for the professional guidance and mentoring I had provided, but better than that, many made the point that they saw Christian principles applied in my decisions and actions. I thought to myself, "That's what work should be about."

My point in sharing all of this is not to impress you, but to note how backward my priorities were. While my trophies were displayed for all to see, evidence of my more important achievements involving the sharing of my Christian beliefs, was locked in my desk drawer in that letter file. My wife, Snookie, loves to make scrapbooks. I first thought about asking her to make one to include those personal tributes for the trophy room. Then I had a better idea; I would just put all those other awards in a closet in the basement.

In this and from other experiences, I have learned that our perception of success often does not match up with God's standards. True success is not measured in terms of dollars, trophies or titles, but instead in the often unrecognized contributions made to others and the inner joy experienced from following God's purpose in life.

> **True success is not measured in terms of dollars, trophies or titles, but instead in the often unrecognized contributions made to others and the inner joy experienced from following God's purpose in life.**

SOLID TO THE CORE

Worldly success is only skin deep. This became clear to me one day while I was observing a new door being installed in a recently constructed area of our building. A hole had been cut in the door for a louver which would allow ventilation of the room. In viewing the cross-section of this door, I noted that its interior was made up of some sort of wood chips that were glued together, and the exterior was just a thin covering of wood. That type of outer surface is called veneer.

Installed, these doors cost approximately $500.00 each, so I thought they would at least be the real thing—solid wood. However, when the door was hung, stained and the hardware attached, you couldn't tell it from a solid wood door. Since I am a woodworker of sorts, I also know that most furniture made today is constructed similarly to that door. It is generally made of plywood or particle board, which also is covered with veneer.

Maybe it's alright for furniture and doors to be artificial inside and real only on the surface. We sometimes view such inventions as progress. We see them as more modern and more efficient. However, there is one problem with this type of construction. When the outer surface is penetrated by a hard blow or bump, then the real composition of the wood is exposed and it becomes obvious that this imitation is not the real thing.

It seems to me that some people are like that door I observed. What you see on the outside camouflages that which is on the inside. In life's journey, we tend to get bumped around a lot, so many times our real selves show despite our efforts to cover them up. When I reflect, I see myself often putting on a front which is not the real me. I personally feel that I spend too much time trying to polish my veneer rather than in attempting to improve my interior substance.

Grady Poulard said it best: "The measure of a man is not determined by his show of outward strength, or the volume of his voice, or the thunder of his action. It is to be seen, rather in terms of the strength of his inner self, in terms of the nature and depth of his commitments, the genuineness of his friendships, the sincerity of his purpose, the quiet courage of his convictions, of his capacity to suffer and his willingness to continue growing up."[9]

I have often had reason to be thankful for the solid, genuine individuals in my life. I just hope one day to earn solid-to-the-core status with others.

> **I have often had reason to be thankful for the solid, genuine individuals in my life. I just hope one day to earn solid-to-the-core status with others.**

"On the outside you appear to people as righteous but on the inside you are full of hypocrisy and wickedness."
—Matthew 23:28

GOING FOR TWO

Successful people go for it! Like many of you, I am an ardent football fan and, in particular, a University of Georgia Bulldog fan. Years ago when Vince Dooley was head coach at Georgia, UGA won an exciting game over the Georgia Tech Yellow Jackets. The score was 29-28 and to win the game, Georgia had to "go for two" with only a couple of minutes left.

A safe and conservative call by the coach would have been to kick the extra point after the final touchdown. If this choice was made, two things could happen; his team would either tie or lose the game (this was prior to the current sudden death rule). By going for two points, a different set of occurrences would follow. They could still lose the game, but they also would have the opportunity of winning it. However, the odds are much greater to lose while attempting the two point conversion instead of kicking the extra point.

Ironically, only two weeks earlier, in a game against Auburn a decision was made by the Georgia coach to tie a ballgame (although admittedly the circumstances were slightly different). Time ran out and the tie resulted in Georgia losing the Southeastern Conference title and a trip to the prestigious Sugar Bowl.

I'm just glad that I'm not a football coach. However, it seems to me that we all face decisions in our lives and jobs which will either result in losing, tying or winning. When facing such choices, my resolution is to always "go for two." Coaches were seldom criticized for losing on the football field while trying to win instead of tie the game.

Life's work is a constant effort toward winning battles for those things that are good and right. There are few fields of endeavor where winning is more important than in a hospital.

> **Life's work is a constant effort toward winning battles for those things that are good and right.**

> *"Whatever your hand finds to do, do it with all your might."*
> —*Ecclesiastes 9: 10*

LEARNING BY LOSING

Success does not mean winning every time. I once had the opportunity to run for a national office in my professional organization. The timing was just right. In fact, if my candidacy did not fly then, I probably would never have this particular opportunity again. I was very excited about the possibility of such an accomplishment and began lining up my support and making all the right political moves to ensure my success in this effort. I had agreement from my board chairman and my wife to offer myself for this high position. Then, after doing all I knew to do, I sat back and waited with great anticipation for my confirmation from the nominating committee.

The chairman called me immediately after the committee had met, and in a kind but direct manner, informed me that someone else would be the nominee. The words felt like a dagger going directly into my heart. With my ego totally deflated, I sat there stunned for a long time. I went to an unrelated meeting that afternoon, but could think only about my defeat. How could this other guy possibly have beaten me? I was more qualified. I was a better politician. I had all the support...I thought. But what I thought didn't count...it was not to be.

Afterwards, one of my most difficult tasks was to tell the folks who had advised and helped me that I had lost. I even thought, "Why did I ever get involved in this anyway? If I had not run, I would not have lost."

It has been a while now, and I can look at this "defeat" much more objectively. In retrospect, it was a great experience. I had the privilege of reading copies of some complimentary letters of endorsement from my friends. I realize that many were exaggerated, but they made me feel really special anyway. I was broadened professionally by the preparation required to seek such an office. I met other colleagues who gave me further insight into our field and profession. And I even became friends with the gentleman who defeated me in the election, and he was a nice person. But more importantly, I probably would now stand a better chance of being victorious in future endeavors. In my mind, I was a better person because of this experience. Boy, what a great privilege it was just to have had the opportunity to participate at this level!

Life is too short and fragile to worry about accomplishments which go unachieved. Instead, we should remember that our future opportunities are endless. You know, all things do work together for good for those whose motivation and purpose is right. In this case, that proved to be especially true. My defeat gave me that extra time to finish a book I had been working on, and more importantly, time to go hunting a few more times with my son before he went off to college. Maybe by trying to be the best we can be, we at least turn out better than we might have been.

> **Life is too short and fragile to worry about accomplishments which go unachieved.**

"And we know that in all things God works for the good of those who love him, who have been called according to his purpose."
—Romans 8:28

NOT JUST OLDER, BUT WISER

Sometimes even age contributes to success. During a visit to our organization by the Joint Commission on the Accreditation of Health-care Organizations (JCAHO), one of the surveyors shared a thought-provoking illustration with us.

Dr. Samuel Joseph, the physician representative on the team, told about a conversation he had with a doctor at another hospital concerning the documentation of a routine surgical procedure. The doctor involved became somewhat irate and stated, "I have been performing this opera-tion the same way since I began practicing medicine, and I have had 30 years of experience."

Dr. Joseph, whom we found to be extremely perceptive, yet quite witty in his manner, replied, "If you have been doing it the same way that long, you haven't had 30 years of experience. You have had one year's experience 30 times."

I went back to my office that day and thought, "Do I really have 30 years of experience under my belt or have I had one year's experience 30 times? Or maybe three year's experience 10 times or five year's experience six times?" Probably among those or some other combinations, I would have found my true amount of work experience. Hopefully, most of my years were full of growth and development. Yet, I'm honest enough to recognize that at times I was stymied, coasting or just downright lazy.

It seems to me that our own personal success, as well as the success of an organization, is largely dependent on the desire of its employees to continually grow and develop professionally. It is interesting to note that after we have experienced growth, we are never quite the same again.

Oliver Wendell Holmes said, "Man's mind stretched to a new idea never goes back to its original dimensions."[10] John Foster Dulles, in relat-ing experience to success, stated, "The measure of success is not whether you have a tough problem to deal with, but whether it's the same prob-lem you had last year."[11]

In terms of personal and professional development, my goal for that next year and every one since (even into retirement) has been to gain a full year's worth of growing experiences. If I can accomplish this,

I will not only be one year older, but also a year wiser. I wish the same for you.

> **In terms of personal and professional development, my goal for that next year and every one since has been to gain a full year's worth of growing experiences.**

"Gray hair is a crown of splendor..."
—*Proverbs 16:31*

A BIG LITTLE GUY

Success is not determined by how big and strong we are. All of us have qualities and talents that are uniquely our own, but I'm sure that there isn't one of us who hasn't wanted to be just like someone else in one way or another. Often, it is what we perceive as our weaknesses that we want to change, but sometimes those very weaknesses are really strengths in disguise. Let me give you an example.

I may have been the world's best sidewalk superintendent because I loved building projects and really enjoyed watching them during the different stages of construction. One day, I was observing the progress on a parking deck being built for our doctors. It was a hot, busy day out there. Forms were being erected, decking and pans were being put in place and concrete trucks were lined up waiting to pour. There must have been twenty-five workmen busy as bees preparing the upper level for concrete. Most of these guys had on tank tops or wore no shirts at all. You could tell that they were in great shape; my kids would say they were "buffed."

But one little fellow seemed out of place in that setting. He was probably a foot shorter than any of the others and lacked all the protruding muscles. Because he was so conspicuously different, I remember thinking to myself, "I wonder how that little guy got a construction job; he must be the owner of the company's son."

As I watched, it became apparent there was a problem. Evidently inside the forms for a main column, the supporting steel rods or some part of the interior framing had slipped out of place. The only choice to remedy the situation seemed to be to disassemble all the forms, but the concrete was beginning to harden in the trucks. Then the foreman called for "Little Joe." They attached him to a rope hoist and lowered him into the column's 18-inch opening, so he could correct the problem. At that moment, it became clear to me why this little guy was part of the team. About five minutes later, he emerged the hero who had saved the day, and work continued on schedule.

After watching all of this, I concluded that maybe success should be measured not so much by our physical attributes, our mental capabilities or even our spiritual maturity, as by the weaknesses and limitations which we have used or overcome while striving to succeed. These, rather than the things that come easy, tend to extract the best that is in us.

A little fellow, who would have probably preferred to be larger and taller, could do something that no one else could do; and as a result, all benefited from his special traits. He turned his weakness into strength. To want to be like everyone else is a human tendency; to desire to be unique and special is the result of divine revelation.

> **To want to be like everyone else is a human tendency; to desire to be unique and special is the result of divine revelation.**

"For when I am weak, then I am strong."
—2 Corinthians 12:10

THE POWER OF BROKENNESS

Honesty and integrity are characteristics of successful people. I had a small figurine of a little old lady on a table in my office. This little statue was a workwoman with a broom and washbasin. She had been in my office so long that I didn't generally notice her unless she was mentioned by someone.

One day I received a call from a housekeeping supervisor who said one of his workers had accidentally knocked the figurine off the table when she was cleaning my office. Its arm had been broken and the housekeeping assistant was very upset about the incident and wanted to pay for it.

Though this may have seemed like a little thing to most people, I was very impressed by the honesty and concern of this person. It would have been so easy just to ignore it and not mentioned what had happened; no one would have ever known. I could even remember times in my own life when I did not face up to mistakes and miscues. After this experience, it seemed to me that there were still a lot of good people in this world and many of them worked in our hospital.

A little super glue totally restored the glass workwoman, and the sensitivity of a housekeeping assistant made me feel good all day. I made a point to meet her and we became friends. In my eyes, she was truly at the top of the organization chart functioning very successfully. It seemed ironic that a working woman broke the figure of a workwoman and because of her honesty a great lesson was delivered.

> **A working woman broke the figure of a workwoman and because of her honesty a great lesson was delivered.**

"Kings take pleasure in honest lips. They value a man (or woman) who speaks the truth."
—Proverbs 16:13

HANDLING ENVY

While some personal attributes foster success, others detract from it. One of those is envy. Unfortunately, from time to time I find myself becoming envious of other folks and their accomplishments. Many of these people have more initials behind their names; many have achieved higher status or advanced further professionally than I did. Many have made more money and drive better cars, and many are just smarter, more articulate and intelligent than I'll ever be.

Interestingly, I used to feel this way when I was bagging groceries as a teenager, and even when I headed a $1.5 billion business, those inner feelings tended to pop up periodically. Evidently it is difficult to remove such destructive, egotistical thoughts from one's mind.

I did receive a little comfort one day when an acquaintance confided that he felt the same way. I wonder if everybody has this tendency from time to time. I was bowled over once when another friend told me that he was envious of me. What made this so overwhelming was the fact that I had been envious of him.

Then I noticed, hanging on the wall in my Mom's den, an embroidered picture of a sunflower with the following inscription: "Bloom Where You Are Planted." That really spoke to me. I said to myself, "Bernie, why are you worrying about where everybody else is instead of trying to be the very best where you are?"

I once heard a preacher use in his sermon an illustration dealing with the universal concern that people have about accepting their stations in life. He said, "A well maintained Ford is a far better means of transportation than a neglected Rolls Royce." In other words, in certain situations the "little folks" may make a more significant contribution than the "big folks."

It seems to me that God made all of us in unique ways, and we each have special talents to offer our organizations as well as to share with others. When I really think about it, I would not change places with anybody because I am special. Therefore, there is no reason to be envious anymore!

> **God made all of us in unique ways, and we each have special talents to offer our organizations as well as to share with others.**

"Let us not become conceited, provoking and envying each other."
—Galatians 5:26

HANDLING FAILURE

When talking about succeeding, we must also address failing. From reading, from listening and from my own personal experience, I have concluded that all of us from time to time have real feelings of failure.

While talking with a doctor, I sensed genuine frustration on his part when he indicated that one of his patients was not responding satisfactorily to the treatment he had prescribed. I remember many times losing a match in a tennis tournament, not getting the job I really wanted, and feeling like I had let my family down when one of them needed my support. If I had kept a count over the years, my failures may have even out-numbered my successes. If you are honest, you might reach the same conclusion in your own situation.

It seems to me that failure can be either a positive or negative force in our lives, depending on how we respond to it. William A. Ward expressed it best when he stated, "Failure should be our teacher, not our undertaker. Failure is delay, not defeat. It is a temporary detour, not a dead-end street."[12]

I once read about a young boy who loved to sketch and draw. He was told by his teachers to stop wasting his time because he had no talent. Instead he just looked at this failure as a challenge to keep working and improving. Finally, this young man's work caught on. His name was Walt Disney. The next time I fail, I'm going to get out my old comic books and read about Mickey Mouse, Pluto and Donald Duck. Failing is part of the process of achieving success; however, giving up is not!

> **Failing is part of the process of achieving success; however, giving up is not!**

"Let us not become weary in doing good, for at the proper time we will reap a harvest if we do not give up."
Galatians 6:9

KEYS TO SUCCESS

Some years ago, I was asked to give the keynote address at the annual meeting of a national health care corporation. This was a real honor and privilege for me, so I attempted to give some extra in-depth thought in preparing for my presentation. I was requested to speak on "being successful in a highly competitive environment."

I did not have to convince anyone that the health care business was highly competitive. Dynamic and chaotic were adjectives that described the industry both then and now. Some had even portrayed health care as being immersed in a gigantic bowl of alphabet soup. To confirm this, I once asked someone to record the initials and acronyms used by those attending a staff meeting. Here were the results: HCFA, HMO, PPO, IPA, CON, SHPA, AHA, GHA, VHA, HCA, AMI, ACHE, PT, OT, RN, PHP, MD, DO, UR, ASAP, PRN, IRA, CCU, ER, OR, ICU, NICU, JCAHO, EDP, HBOC, MHA, EMT, RT, ET, SMSA, PPS, DME, ADS, AIDS. Sometimes it seemed that we were playing a crucial game of organizational scrabble as we attempted to sort out the right combinations of operational activities which lead to success.

In our search for organizational success, I feel that we often approach the task backwards. We work so hard to reach institutional goals and objectives that at times individual development, satisfaction and recognition go lacking. Yet, from what I have observed over the years, successful individuals make successful organizations. Certainly an interdependence exists between individual and organizational success, yet over and over again I have seen losing teams become winners, poor departments excel, and dying companies prosper when just one successful individual is placed in the right position. In my estimation, successful individuals make successful organizations far more often than successful organizations make successful individuals.

This leads to the conclusion that a key to success in any enterprise is identifying, attracting, employing and retaining successful individuals. If it's that simple, some may ask, "Why aren't all organizations successful?" There are probably many reasons why organizations fail to attract successful individuals, but here are just a few: first, there are not enough successful individuals to go around; second, the ones that are already successful are often unaffordable; and third, it's difficult to recognize the individuals who will become successful as they mature. It seemed to me that if there were ways to identify potentially successful individuals, an organization would come close to ensuring its success.

I think that I have discovered certain clues to identify individuals who are going to be successful, and I'm going to share them with you.

An older man once told me the key to success was to "keep your priorities straight." I readily agreed but wondered, "What should those priorities be?" Along the same line, a colleague of mine used an interesting technique when he interviewed a candidate for a job. He always asked, "What are the three top priorities in your life?" His experience in doing this proved so effective in evaluating an applicant that I started asking the same question. I firmly believe that success in life is directly related to one's priorities.

Here are the three priorities I am convinced will lead to a successful life. I'll start with what I think is the third most important: your *job*.

I honestly felt that I had the best job in the world. This attitude stemmed from the fact that my job was important; it had purpose and I gained satisfaction from what I was doing. But above all, my own particular purpose or calling (what I believe that I'm really here for) was embodied in my specific job. Stated another way, my purpose was the same as our organization's purpose.

Because of this positive attitude toward my job, I was one of the best salesmen in the world for the organization. A few may have been able to sell it better than I could, but that was only because they were more talented in salesmanship, not because they were more committed.

Because my job was one of my top priorities, I really wanted to do it well. I gave it my best and owed it my loyalty, for it provided me a livelihood and means of self-fulfillment. I hope that you realize by now that I loved my job!

Some may say, "But I didn't have as good a job as you had. You were high up in the organization." To that I reply, the "quality" of any job has nothing to do with its rank or status, but instead with the attitude of the one who fills it. We had folks who loved their jobs as much or more than I did at all levels, not because any individual job was perfect but because it was important to them and the organization.

It seems to me that every organization has a purpose. All jobs within it should have a similar purpose and people hired to fill those jobs should have that same purpose. For heaven's sake, if your job is not in keeping with your purpose, go find another one. My wife has worked outside our home but mostly has been a stay-at-home mom. I have always felt that she had a more important job than mine. Her organization was called "our Christian home" and she did a great job because it was one of her top priorities. (By the way, since my retirement she has reminded me that she is the CEO of the home.)

I guess that one of the main reasons my job was one of my top priorities was because it provided me with a place where I could "professionally serve and personally care," and no one had a higher calling than that. People who have their *jobs* as one of their top priorities have taken one step toward success.

I believe the second most important priority is *family.* To the traditional family member, one with a spouse and/or children, brothers, sisters, parents, etc., this is an obvious choice. In my own case, I cannot think of anything in this world that is more important to me than my immediate family. In my mind, probably the worst thing that could happen to me personally would be to lose a family member through death, debilitating illness or a broken relationship.

But why should a family be so important? From a practical standpoint, let me suggest a few reasons. First, individuals who care about those at home will also tend to care about others in different settings, such as the workplace. Second, families are teams; therefore, family members learn teamwork. Third, basic values are generally learned best in a family setting. Finally, family life carries great responsibility, which fosters wisdom and understanding and helps one to grow to maturity.

Psychologists have long insisted that a healthy family environment is one of the greatest support and stabilizing mechanisms available to any person. Of course, I realize that bad things can happen in the best of families. However, I still contend that an attitude of love and respect towards one's personal family despite difficulties and problems, is a necessity in the search for success.

In the context of this discussion, I would like to broaden the term "family." Most of us also have church, school, civic, community and and/or professional families. For example, we often referred to our organization as the hospital family. (An interesting note: the only thing all my different families have in common is that I am a member of each.) Generally, folks don't have much trouble putting themselves high on their own priority scale, but to bestow such lofty status to others is something contrary to human nature. It seems to me that it is much easier to give others a higher priority rating if we think of all those with whom we live, work and associate as "family."

In short, those who are successful tend not to put *me* before *thee*, but to include both as *we*. If *family* is second place on our list of priorities, we have taken another step toward success.

Now I want to tell you what I honestly believe to be the first priority of a successful person – *God.*

Why is one's relationship with God so important? First, without the existence of God, we as individuals would be here only by chance, for no particular purpose. I would have a tough time believing that there is nothing more to life than just a game of chance. Second, merely to believe that God exists does not ensure success. However, true success begins when a personal relationship develops with God through his son, Jesus Christ. Let me give you an example of what I mean. My preceptor when I was a hospital administration resident was one of the outstanding health care executives in the country. He was recognized nationally and internationally for his contributions to our profession. However, I didn't learn by knowing of his reputation, but rather from the personal contact and exposure I had observing him function as the chief executive of a major institution. Third, every successful person needs someone to serve as a continual counselor, sustainer and role model. I was blessed to have one of the best fathers in the world (and mothers also, for that matter). He helped me when I needed help; he advised me when I needed advice;

he set an example for me to follow; and most importantly, he always loved me despite my many shortcomings and faults. My dad left me a precious legacy, but he is gone, as all of us will go in our turn. Because of my own weaknesses, inadequacies and insecurities, I need the eternal source of support that only God can provide.

Finally, to belong gives a person a sense of security and confidence. One of the most publicized individuals for many years has been Prince Charles of Great Britain. Accounts of his activities appear on television and in magazines and newspapers around the world. The reason he receives so much attention is the fact that he is son of the Queen. If that is the case, how much more special are we, who are sons and daughters of a "King," the King of the Universe, God our Heavenly Father. In other words, we are important because we belong to God and he "don't make no mistakes."

I have been a church-goer all my life. Such behavior was expected from a preacher's kid. But I began to find genuine happiness and fulfillment when I discovered some years ago that God is alive not just on Sunday, but all through the week. As a result of this revelation, my job became a ministry, and for the first time I began to sense real success in my own life.

Some may argue, "I know people who are rich, travel in high society, know the right people, boss a lot of folks, get their pictures in the paper...are ultra successful, and they could care less about God!" My response to them is, "Are they truly successful?" Remember, true success is not measured in terms of dollars, trophies or titles, but instead in the often unrecognized contributions made to others and the inner joy experienced from following God's purpose in life.

In summary, the right priorities are the keys to success. I believe one's job (including the job of homemaker for some), family and God are the three top priorities of a successful person. The *job* provides a means of success; the *family* provides a reason for success; and *God* provides the way to success. I wish for each of you true success in your life's journey.

**The *job* provides a means of success;
the *family* provides a reason for success;
and *God* provides the way to success.**

"Seek first His kingdom and His righteousness, and all these things will be given to you as well." (Matthew 6:33)

DISCOVERING TRUE SUCCESS

"Let another praise you, and not your own mouth; someone else and not your own lips." (Proverbs 27:2)

Questions for Further Study and Discussion

1. What is your definition of success? What is God's definition of it? What is earthly success? How do these definitions differ?

2. Do you know some solid-to-the-core people? What makes them that way?

3. Are you a risk taker? In what areas of your life would you take risks? In what areas would you not?

4. Have you ever lost at something that ended up being a win? Have you ever won at something that ended up being a loss?

5. Do you have 30 (or whatever) years' experience in your work? Or, do you have one year's experience 30 times? Explain your answer.

6. Have you ever known someone different from you and others who used that uniqueness to help the organization succeed? Do you have any unique qualities that make you valuable to the organization?

7. How does individual honesty and integrity affect the success of an organization?

8. Is envy one of your character traits? How can you remove this destructive characteristic from your thoughts and actions?

9. Does fear of failure hinder your potential? In your mind, how do your failures compare with your successes in size and scope?

10. What are your top three priorities in life?

TEACHING AND BEING TEACHABLE

"He guides the humble in what is right and teaches them his way."
—Psalm 25:9

Someone once asked me to describe a "leader." I wanted to make it simple and understandable, so I used this analogy. A leader is the combination of a coach and a quarterback on a football team. Coaching is the leader's sideline function and quarterbacking is the on-field activity. Most good coaches played their game at an earlier time in their lives, and most good quarterbacks take the role of coaches on the field. The coach is generally considered a teacher, and the quarterback is viewed as a student of the coach's system and strategy who leads the team throughout the game. I say all this to make the point that a leader must not only be a teacher, but just as importantly, must also be teachable. I once heard a leader of leaders indicate that one of the most valuable attributes that those who worked with him should have was to be teachable – willing to continually learn without an arrogant, know-it-all attitude. In recent years, books have even been written that promote the concept of "a learning organization," which emphasizes the need for all to be teachable throughout its ranks.

> **A leader must not only be a teacher, but just as importantly, must also be teachable.**

The fact that I entitled this work *"Lessons Learned"* implies that this author has been taught something he wants to share. Hopefully, I have done that – shared with you some basic lessons I have learned. As I have told my stories, you have already been introduced to some of my "coaches" along the way. In concluding this section, I would like to introduce you to a few more of those who significantly influenced both my work and my life.

BERNARD TAUGHT ME TO CARE
(Written in 1989)

I wrote the following while on an emotional roller coaster:

I've just been to visit a patient who suffered a serious heart attack. I'm so glad I had the opportunity to spend an extended period of time with him because he has been such a special person to me over the years. I would like to share a few personal observations concerning this individual who has helped me shape some of my own principles and values. This gentleman had just passed his eightieth birthday on the fourth of July. When he was young, he thought the fireworks each year were for him. After he was grown, he developed a great taste for beautiful women. He married one of the most attractive and lovely ladies I have ever known. (Incidentally, they celebrated their fiftieth wedding anniversary two years ago.) And though he had one son, his claim to fame was his three beautiful daughters (I mean they were all good-looking and had a special glow that went more than skin-deep). In short, he was a great family man.

His profession was preaching. He moved around serving churches large and small and held several administrative posts during his career. But he was known mainly as a pastor. He and his wife were the first people I ever knew who professionally served and personally cared constantly. That's the reason our organizational slogan is so meaningful to me. To be honest, I don't believe I have seen anyone else do it better than the two of them. When a need was there, they were, too. A friend at the hospital commented to me during my visit, "I've never known anyone who loves to love others as much as he does."

> **When a need was there, they were, too.**

He had a great sense of humor and did some amusing things from time to time. For example, I remember going on a particular fishing trip with him. We arrived at the lake on Sunday afternoon, but he didn't believe in fishing on Sunday. I was grown at the time and didn't see anything wrong with it, so I fished late in the afternoon. I caught a six pound catfish and carried it up to the cabin to clean and show it off. When I returned to the lake, he was sitting on the dock watching a pole hanging over the side. Of course, it was not in his hand, so I can't swear he was fishing on Sunday.

He was tough and believed in discipline. When I was growing up, I was not scared of him, but I really respected his authority because he used it quite effectively. As an administrator today, I look back on some of the principles of authority, responsibility and accountability that he practiced. There is no doubt I'm better at my job as the result of observing him.

In my eyes, this man was famous. By this I mean so many people knew him, and once they met him they never forgot him. This was always helpful to me because he would become a topic of conversation with people throughout the area who knew and appreciated him. I learned in many cases that he had assisted them with some problem in the past.

In summary, I would say that he was the most special man I have ever known. I just hope one day folks will remember me as fondly as I remember him.

As I left his room that day, I asked for the most accurate evaluation of his condition. "He's critical and in heart failure and it doesn't look good," the doctor said.

Please forgive me for being so personal, but I felt the need to share a few thoughts with you about my dad.

Rev. Bernard L. Brown, Sr.
1909-1989

"Listen, my son, to your father's instruction..."
—Proverbs 1:8

ELIZABETH TAUGHT ME TO LOVE
(Written in 1994)

One of my favorite places in the whole world is Epworth-by-the-Sea. Epworth is a church-related (United Methodist) conference center located on St. Simons Island, Georgia. It's so special to me because I have been going there since I was a child. Every time I'm down at Epworth and St. Simons, I visit with Elizabeth, who has worked there for more than twenty years. During my last visit, she told me that she was retiring from her job as Director of Housekeeping Services. (This was her second career, her first being that of a homemaker and wife of a Methodist preacher.) Elizabeth is seventy-five years old, but is a beautiful lady who looks to me like she's in her early sixties.

It seems like I have known her forever. I have admired her work ethic and commitment to her job and responsibilities. As Housekeeping Director she would never leave until she was sure every room was cleaned and every bed was made. Her ability to manage and supervise workers was amazing. Her folks not only responded to her leadership but they all loved and respected her. In the time I have known her, I cannot remember anyone ever saying a disparaging word about her, nor have I ever heard her talk negatively about anyone else.

Even though Elizabeth, like most women of her generation, did not go to college, I consider her to be one of the most brilliant and wise individuals I have ever known. Some of the principles I have watched her preach and practice include the following:

- Family should always be among one's top priorities.
- Bloom where you're planted.
- Look for good in every situation.
- Leave a good impression wherever you go.
- Help others reach their potential.
- People are more important than things.
- God is great; God is good.
- I love you unconditionally!

I love you unconditionally!

These are but a few of the many, many lessons you learn quickly from just being around her.

Once in a recent phone conversation with Elizabeth, I was sharing my delight that my son Jeff was soon to receive his second master's degree. I was expressing my amazement that he had accomplished such a feat, remembering some of his struggles during elementary school, high school and college. She laughed and shared with me a conversation she had with my father many years earlier. When I got my first real job in a hospital, he exclaimed to her, "Did you ever think Bernie would amount to anything like this?" To this, she indignantly answered, "I certainly did! I believe he could be President of the United States if he wanted to be!"

By now, I'm sure you realize why Elizabeth is one of the most special people in the whole world to me. What a role model she is! Her friends call her Elizabeth; her workers call her Mrs. Brown. I call her "Mom."

"...and do not forsake your mother's teaching."
—Proverbs 1:8

DAVID TAUGHT ME ENDURANCE

Just before I retired, I took up an old habit—I gave blood during the employee blood drive. It used to be something I did regularly, and I wore my 7-gallon pin with pride. But like many, I somehow got out of the habit of regular blood donations. It felt good to resume doing something so simple, and yet so vital to those in need.

This reminded me of a story about a very special gift of blood. I heard it during a lunch with a personal friend, who during his childhood fought a valiant bout with polio. Many younger folks will not remember when polio was the scourge of childhood, but those of us who were kids before the advent of the polio vaccine recall how scared our parents were of the very word *polio*. If a youngster in the neighborhood contracted the disease, our parents would forbid us to go to the public swimming pools because it was feared that it could be transmitted through water. Some kids weren't even allowed to go outdoors for a week or two because of the fear the germs could be airborne. Polio was a crippler and a killer that blighted many young lives.

Stricken at age 12, my friend was very seriously ill. In addition to paralysis of his limbs, his ability to breathe was endangered. In the room with him was an iron lung in case it was needed in a hurry. (An iron lung was a breathing device that resembled a big metal tube. The tube covered a patient from chin to feet and assisted with breathing when polio caused severe lung damage. Some children even lived the rest of their lives in an iron lung.)

We can only imagine the torment my friend and his parents went through during the critical stages of his illness. His memories of that time were spotty, but little boys tend to remember being stuck by needles so he does recall that a lot of blood was drawn. Fortunately, he never did need that iron lung, but he was left with some permanent physical impairment.

However, there is another side to this story that reaches beyond the tragedy of the disease. He learned later that some of the blood that they drew from him was sent for research purposes to a laboratory headed by

Dr. Jonas Salk and was used to help develop the polio vaccine. Despite his personal suffering, he now has a special pride in knowing that generations of children are free of polio, thanks in part to his blood.

I don't think my friend and former co-worker would mind if I revealed his name. All at the hospital at that time probably could guess that I am referring to David Malden, who directed the system's purchasing function. Anyone who knows David is aware of the fact that he never let polio or its lasting effects define his life. He was a valued employee of the organization for over 20 years and has a wonderful family. David has lived a full, productive, inspirational life, knowing that his suffering helped bring a cure that is of inestimable value to countless others.

Blood is something that we all must have. It is priceless and to share it is an act of sacrificial love. We may not all have the opportunity to be a part of medical history. Some of us cannot give blood for clinical reasons. But we all can give our talents and skills and yes, even our love to those we serve. That focus is something we must take special care to keep in our changing world. David gave his blood, but beyond that he also stayed on the path to a very productive life serving others.

> **We all can give our talents and skills and yes, even our love to those we serve. That focus is something we must take special care to keep in our changing world.**

"This is my blood…which is poured out for many."
—Mark 14:24

A CHICKEN TAUGHT ME, YOU CAN DO IT!

I once had the privilege of traveling in what was then the Soviet Union with a group of hospital administrators who were observing the health care system in that country. Even though this was the opportunity of a lifetime, I find that I can remember less and less about my experience there as time goes by. Then periodically something triggers my memory about certain places or things and it all comes back to me. For example, a television mini-series on Peter the Great reminded me of our visit to Leningrad (now St. Petersburg).

Those who know me personally recognize that I am not the most intellectual or perceptive individual in the world. Therefore, I tend to relate to the very basic, simple things of life. The reason I mention this is that I saw something one day that carried me back to my memories of our Russian tour.

While driving in a rural area of southern Georgia on my way to join my hunting buddy, I rode by a farmhouse and saw a chicken walking along the top of a fence like it was on a tightrope. This reminded me of a visit to the world-famous Moscow Circus. There in a traditional big-top tent, I saw one of the greatest circus performances you could imagine. You won't believe this, but one of the star attractions was a trained chicken. In pure amazement, I watched that chicken ride a bike, count, dance, sing, and do things I have only seen done by trained dogs, lions, tigers and bears.

I guess the reason this seemed so astonishing was that I had never imagined a chicken could do such things. This was totally out of character. In my mind, chickens were only good for eggs and frying.

It seems to me that there are some folks around who are much like that trained chicken. We never dreamed that they could be trained to do anything. We never expected them to accomplish so much. Surely, success in their field of endeavor was not anticipated.

I still cannot believe that some years ago a little five-foot-seven-inch tall basketball player won the NBA's slam dunk contest. The former Atlanta Hawk guard, Spud Webb, is even more amazing to me than that Moscow Circus chicken. Some of the other *"trained chickens"* of the world include these:

A deaf composer–Ludwig von Beethoven;
A slow learner–Albert Einstein;
A blind musician–Ray Charles;
An octogenarian painter–Grandma Moses;
A victim of racial prejudice–George Washington Carver.

Most of us tend to conform ourselves to society's expectations instead of venturing a bit out of character toward something special and unique. My conclusion is that doing our thing in life's center ring is far better than just waiting to be plucked.

> **Doing our thing in life's center ring is far better than waiting to be plucked.**

Some might be perplexed that I consider a trained chicken as one of my coaches. But I consider a whole host of people and things that have taught me lessons to be my coaches!
(Note: This piece originally appeared in my column titled, "It Seems to Me..." in the hospital's newsletter. A few days later I received this letter.)

> *Dear Mr. Brown, It seems to me... that you might have to add another "trained chicken" to your list*
> *Bill Leydecker, Windy Hill Food Service, has been with you for almost four years now. He's married and has a three-year-old daughter. His wife has epilepsy and is also a slow learner, so he walks home for lunch every day to check up on things. He also does a majority of the cooking at home.*
> *As you can imagine, when we received the enclosed "Discharge Summary" (indicating Bill's birth defects and deficiencies), we were devastated. Fortunately for us, and Bill, we had five more children. Bill never understood his disabilities for many years, and therefore, never accepted them as a reason for not attempting to live a normal life. He learned from his siblings.*
> *We are very proud of Bill and hope you are also to have him on your staff.*
> *Sincerely, W. K Leydecker (Bill's father)* [13]

"My grace is sufficient for you, for my power is made perfect in weakness."
—*2 Corinthians 12:9*

DOCTOR KAISER TAUGHT ME, "NOW WHAT?"

When I was working for pay, I was constantly attending meetings, seminars and conferences aimed at assisting the participants to be more effective in their jobs. I used to make it a point to bring back at least one important lesson from each of these and put it into practice. Unfortunately, not all the meetings produced a "keeper."

At one of those meetings, the speaker cited a quote from the well-known author and futurist, Dr. Leland Kaiser, which gave me a real "keeper" to bring home. It was so good that I made a point to adopt it into my philosophy of life and work, and I used it often. This is how it went: When a crisis (either real or perceived) first occurs, ask, "So what?" Then ask, "Now what?"[14]

If you think about those words a little bit, they are not as flippant as they may seem at first. Keeping perspective in the heat of a crisis is always a good idea. If I ask myself, "So what? Who or what is really hurt by this? What is affected? What will change, and will the change be positive or negative?" I will often find that the "crisis" is no more than an inconvenience, a personal embarrassment, or maybe even an opportunity to think of things in a different way that will ultimately lead to improvement. When I manage to put a little distance between myself and the problem, I'm apt to find it's not such a big deal after all. Sometimes all that is required is to laugh and forget it.

But if action is needed, we should then ask ourselves, "Now what?" No matter how serious a challenge may be, it's always good to think of how we can move forward. Did I make a mistake? It will do no good for me to wallow in self-blame, beat myself up or (even worse) try to find ways to avoid responsibility. It's far better if I ask myself, "Okay, what should I do next?" That forces me to take a step back from the problem and look at it objectively as I plan my course of action.

I have taken the liberty to add one more question to the others. "Learned what?" This may be the hardest question to deal with in the heat of crisis, but in learning from adversity, one may be able to avoid repeating it. When they add to our understanding, even the most hurtful and negative experiences can turn into opportunities for personal growth and improvement.

It seems to me that my time was well spent at that particular meeting. If I don't remember another thing that was said, I will never forget: *"So what?" "Now what?"* (and my addition) *"Learned what?"* I hope this philosophy will be as helpful to you as it has been to me.

> **"So what?"**
> **"Now what?"**
> **"Learned what?"**

"Listen to advice and accept instruction and in the end you will be wise."
—*Proverbs 19:20*

DON TAUGHT ME HOPE

Several years ago I was asked to contribute to a daily devotional book my church was publishing for its members during the Christmas season. The topic I was assigned was *"hope."* As I thought about what I could say on the subject, Don Logan came to mind. Don was the President of one of the local hospital systems which was a part of the larger system that I headed. He had fought cancer for several years before his death. Watching his courage and his will to enjoy every minute of life was inspiring to me. This is what I wrote after consulting with him during his heroic fight.

When I think of hope, I think of my good friend and colleague, Don Logan, because he seems to possess it in abundance. I asked him how he maintains such a positive attitude in his current situation. He answered in one word: "Hope." "What is happening to me," he continued, "will happen to everyone at some time. I think my job right now is to keep on keeping on. I'm going to make my contributions as best I can and hold on to my sense of purpose. Somehow God is raising me above my circumstances to be able to do that."

135

I once heard that you can live forty days without food, three days without water, eight minutes without air, but not one second without hope.

Don, President of Southern Regional Health System, recently told me that his cancer has resurfaced and he is in intense chemotherapy. During the past three years he has battled this illness with unflagging enthusiasm for life. Thanks, Don, for personifying the power of hope.

And thank you, God, for giving us friends like Don to teach us the true meaning of hope.

> **You can live forty days without food, three days without water, eight minutes without air, but not one second without hope.**

In my last conversation with Don we talked candidly about his grave condition. We always ended our phone calls by saying, "See you at the board meeting if I don't see you before." This time he said, "If I don't see you at the board meeting next week, I'll see you in heaven." He died on the day of the meeting.

"Be joyful in hope, patient in affliction..."
—*Romans 12:12*

LOUISE'S TREE TAUGHT ME SACRIFICE

An annual fundraising project of the Kennestone Hospital Volunteers was the lighting of the *"Love Light Tree."* Lights were purchased in honor and memory of individuals throughout the community. Incidentally, during the first ten years this program held every Christmas raised more than $250,000 to support numerous activities within the hospital.

One year this project was especially meaningful to me because, for the first time, a "live" tree was used. There is a very interesting story about this tree which I would like to share with you.

In 1976, prior to her retirement, Louise Brown Wable, our first Director of Volunteers, was honored by the volunteer organization with the planting of a tree on our campus. Before the tree could mature, we were forced to move it down to a spot on the corner of the hospital property to make room for an addition to the facility. The tree did not fare nearly as well in its new location because it was shaded by several large sycamore trees. As a result, the tribute intended for Louise seemed somewhat diminished. However, in time a strange series of events occurred which restored the organization's expression of love and appreciation for Louise.

For the tenth anniversary of the Love Light Tree project, the Volunteers built a patio and planted a permanent live tree instead of placing a cut tree on top of the portico in front of the building. A deodara cedar tree was especially chosen and placed in its freshly landscaped setting. Unfortunately, the new tree seemed to dwarf Louise's spruce, which sat directly behind it on a relatively barren site. When I first noticed the contrast between the two trees, I worried about it because I didn't want Louise to feel that our esteem for her had in any way lessened.

As it turned out, my worry was unwarranted, for the issue would be resolved in a very unusual and unexpected way. Soon after the new patio and tree were in place, I drove around in front of the building to see how it looked to those passing by. To my chagrin, Louise's little tree behind it was gone. Upset, I called to chastise the contractor for cutting down this loving remembrance for this special lady.

To my surprise, I learned that it had not been intentionally removed. Instead, the tree happened to be directly in the path of a runaway automobile with two small children inside. It had kept the car from careening over the hill into the street and probably saved the children's lives. The impact, however, killed the tree.

At the next lighting of the live Love Light Tree, I was asked by the Volunteers to announce that a plaque was being installed at its base noting that this tree (deodar cedar) would from that time on live there in honor of Louise Brown Wable.

This was especially significant to me personally because Louise was one of the first people I met when I came to Kennestone twenty years earlier, and she was one of our most loyal and supportive managers. She was Louise Brown when I came. Her first husband had died and she remarried later. Though we were not actually related but had the same last name, I called her "mom," and she called me "son."

It seemed appropriate for me to paraphrase Matthew 10:39 here: The tree that loses its life for the sake of others will live forever.

> **The tree that loses its life for the sake of others will live forever.**

"...a longing fulfilled is a tree of life."
—Proverbs 13:12

DOCTOR CHARLIE TAUGHT ME COURAGE

Some years ago, a doctor on our medical staff dropped me a thoughtful note and shared an insight he had gained over the years. Let me, in turn, share it with you.

I was reading your recent column...and it reminded me of a remark read or heard somewhere in the past. It said that "courage and bravery are not the absence of fear but rather the mastery and control of fear." I used to worry about starting an operation without complete and unshakeable confidence that I could do it better than anyone else. And then I found out that starting an operation without an intelligent appreciation of the hazards—with a little bit of fear, if you will—was a bit foolish and that the real trick was to overcome that apprehension and perform well in spite of it. Perhaps that thought can occupy another of your columns sometime. I would be certain that many of your employees— particularly when they first start—come to work with an uneasy feeling that they are not quite up to the job.

I thought about developing this idea further, but found that I couldn't express it nearly as well as Dr. Charlie Underwood had. Like Dr. Underwood, I can recall the fear of the first step, the unknown, and other hazards in personal ventures. Before a ball game begins, an athlete can almost hyperventilate from apprehension. During a musical introit, a soloist can almost lose her voice because of an anxiety attack. And now I know that even surgeons' hands can be a bit shaky before the initial incision. Perhaps the lesson in all this is that such reactions are normal and healthy. I would not want a surgeon cutting on me who didn't exhibit such courage.

To those who are truly courageous, the appreciation of one's capabilities should include the recognition of one's fears. I now realize that real courage is the wisdom to fear what ought to be feared, and not to fear what ought not to be feared. Fear may be a bit like cholesterol; a little of it is good, but too much can be fatal.

> **Real courage is the wisdom to fear what ought to be feared, and not to fear what ought not to be feared.**

My thanks to my good friend, Charlie Underwood, for sharing this with me. It is good to know that I'm not the only one who has a healthy case of good fear from time to time.

"The fear of the Lord is the beginning of wisdom..."
—Psalm 111:10

KENNESTONE TAUGHT ME THE DIFFERENCE

The wisest people I have known over the years are folks who know "the difference." In addition to knowing the difference between right and wrong and good and bad, they can instinctively distinguish the difference between those things that are ever-changing and those that never change. Interestingly, a great institution taught me this lesson through the origin of its name.

Even though the last few years of my career were in a corporate setting, I spent most of my time and gained most of my work experience as the CEO of one of the hospitals in our system. Kennestone is one of the largest hospitals in the state of Georgia and is the flagship facility of the WellStar Health System. In my mind, it is one of the best hospitals in the world.

The original building was constructed in 1950 on a hill just north of downtown Marietta, Georgia. It was given an unusual name because of its setting. Kennestone was named for the two mountains which it sits between: Kennesaw Mountain where a famous civil war battle took place and Stone Mountain, a famous tourist attraction in northeast Atlanta.

One day while inspecting an addition to the facility, I was up on the roof. For the first time I noticed the contrast between the two natural structures from which the hospital drew its name. Kennesaw Mountain had on its fall coat; it was beautiful with many autumn colors of orange and red. This made me realize that the mountain behind us constantly changes as the seasons of the year come and go. Then I looked at Stone Mountain out in front of the hospital. It looked as it always does: gray rock exhibiting massiveness and strength. Its appearance never changes.

If we look deeply enough, many times we find hidden meaning in our surroundings. Could it be that life is made up of contrasts? Parts of it are ever changing like the foliage on Kennesaw Mountain, yet other aspects of our existence—certain principles and truths—never change, just like that mountain of stone. Those who are truly wise know the difference.

> **Parts of life are ever changing, yet other aspects of our existence – certain principles and truths – never change.**

My own career attests to these contrasts. I entered the field of health care administration before the enactment of Medicare and retired after the introduction of managed care. What changes I experienced! However, one thing never changed during it all – my calling to professionally serve and personally care.

"Jesus Christ is the same yesterday, today and forever."
—Hebrews 13:9

TEACHING AND BEING TEACHABLE

"He guides the humble in what is right and teaches them his way."
—*Psalm 25:9*

Questions for Further Study and Discussion

1. Are you good at coaching (teaching) others? Are you coachable (teachable)?

2. Have you ever known anyone who seemed totally committed to serving and caring? What was his or her profession? Did you have a good male role model?

3. In your memory, who was the first person who showed you unconditional love? Did you have a good female role model?

4. Do you know someone who has a disability yet seems oblivious to that limitation? Do you even forget about it after a while?

5. Have you ever worked with any "trained chickens?" How do they look at themselves?

6. When faced with a crisis or significant problem of some type, do you say to yourself, "So what" then ask, "Now what" and afterwards inquire "Learned what?"

7. What is you definition of "hope?" How did you learn about hope?

8. How would you define sacrifice? Have you ever known someone whom you felt would give his or her life for you or someone else?

9. Do you consider courage as the absence of fear? How does one deal with fear that occurs prior to performing any act of courage?

10. In your personal and professional lives are there ever-changing and never-changing components? Give examples of each.

8

WAR STORIES

"For though we live in the world, we do not wage war as the world does."
—*2 Corinthians 1:3*

I tend to divide the human life cycle into three stages. The first is primarily dedicated to *learning*. The second phase is devoted to *earning*, and the final one is spent *yearning*. I am now in the yearning stage. I seem to covet a second chance on certain things and wish I had been a better leader and made a more significant contribution. This stage of life is a reflective time, a period when we look back and evaluate the true significance and purpose of our lives thus far and long for this last stage to remain productive and meaningful.

The sum of our experiences, be they good or bad, tends to shape and mold us as persons. We bask in our few great successes and lament the obvious failures, but most fall somewhere in between these two extremes. Perhaps it is important to evaluate not only the great and obvious milestones, but also the many less significant experiences that contribute to the growth of our character in ways we may not fully recognize. I have come to realize that the outcome of these – whether in our private or professional lives – hinges on relationships. Certainly that was true in our organization. Struggles and conflicts in human and organizational relationships are what I classify as war stories. Perhaps these tough times can be more objectively analyzed and described during the "yearning" stage of life. It may even be therapeutic to perform a post mortem on some of our life's classic battles.

War is not fun, particularly if you are one of the primary combatants, but it is a part of life, like it or not. Though war has a negative connotation, there are times when it has a positive result not only for the victor but also for the defeated. Interestingly, there are even times when a winner and a loser are difficult to identify, or to lose is actually to win and vice versa. In addition to win/lose, there is win/win and lose/lose. I guess that I won, as well as lost, my share, but what was most important was whether I learned and grew through the course of the war.

> **I won, as well as lost, my share, but what was most important was whether I learned and grew through the course of the war.**

In sharing the examples that follow, I have also attempted to gain the perspective of those with whom I fought. Today, I number them all as friends even though at the time of these encounters, I considered them foes.

MY WAKE UP CALL—NO CONFIDENCE

It was a routine monthly meeting of the hospital's medical staff executive committee. During my 20-plus years of tenure, I had attended more than 200 such meetings. I wouldn't say the meetings were a snooze exactly – anyone who works with physicians knows that they can be a volatile bunch – but maybe I was running on automatic pilot that night. My full attention was engaged, however, when just before adjournment, an unexpected item was brought forth under "new business." One of the newer, less vocal members of the committee took the floor and said, "I make a motion that we pass a vote of 'no confidence' in the hospital's administration." This occurred without any obvious provocation, but the adoption of such a resolution was considered the "kiss of death" for someone in my position. A similar action had resulted in the termination of a CEO in another local hospital a few months earlier. Fortunately from my standpoint, the president of the staff ruled the motion out of order and set up a committee to study the issues that had led to it.

To me this was a declaration of war. My retaliation was swift. I remember spending half that night preparing a letter which was fired off the next morning to everyone involved with copies to all my board members. I vehemently expressed disappointment, anger and accusations of a conspiracy to professionally destroy me. To make matters worst, rumors of my demise which began internally ultimately reached the pages of the local business journal. (A column in the *Atlanta Business Chronicle* was titled "Brown under fire from Kennestone medical staff"). In other words, this became somewhat of a public issue. Without going into detail, the next few weeks and months were very uncomfortable and unpleasant, and it was obvious that some legitimate problems existed which had led to this attempted coup. Many physicians and my entire board expressed confidence in me, but still this caused a significant division within the institution and particularly in the medical staff which is so crucial to organizational success. The board chair appointed a joint committee to resolve issues which were of concern.

Unfortunately, my personal and professional turmoil was accompanied by some industry phenomena which were just as tumultuous. The major prestigious university medical center in town was in merger conversation with the most feared corporate for-profit health care giant. This would have given our direct competitors tremendous advantage if this marriage had been consummated. Additionally, a storm that started in California had moved through the Midwest and was approaching our city and state. It had been given the ominous name "managed care," which was both feared and hated by our physicians. In retrospect, I now can sense that some of the frustration directed at me was the result of the chaotic environment in which we found ourselves. I guess that my sin to my detractors was that I was not adequately leading our organization through these storms.

Time helped heal my wounded ego and at a point I regained my perspective. I was able to view this constructively as a wake-up call. It caused me to take a long, critical look at myself and ask some soul-searching questions. Was it time for me to go? Had I become too set in my ways? Was I willing to take risks at this stage of my career? What did I want my professional legacy to be? After leading a great hospital organization for so many years, I found myself at a crossroad. I never contemplated professional suicide, but I did question my own ability to continue to provide effective leadership. However, I fell back on a philosophy of one of my first bosses in this field. He openly subscribed to the belief that he could not contribute to the success of the institution if he wasn't around. This survival mentality was not one that I had consciously followed in the past. But I had too much invested in what I considered a great organization to give it all up just because it was getting hot in the kitchen. Instead, I decided that I would attempt to become a better cook.

Many lessons come from an experience such as this. We probably learn more when functioning in a war zone than in the comfort of our normal peaceful existence. At least that is the way it has been for me. Here are a few thoughts I have, now that I am in the yearning stage of life.

First, wartime always results in *suffering*. We tend to think of ourselves as invincible. However, I now admit that I suffered both personally and professionally, at times to the point of despair. Even if criticism is not justified in your mind, it still hurts. Second, the suffering, however, had some benefits. It caused me to rethink, to reload, and to rededicate myself to my job. I needed to continuously grow professionally and to adapt to an ever changing environment. I learned *perseverance* as never before.

Third, experiences like this build *character*. In retrospect, I am not proud of how I conducted myself in every aspect of this encounter. However, the fact that I now recognize my mistakes and weaknesses in this regard gives me some comfort that my character and values were strengthened by this traumatic event.

And finally, the post-war period developed into a new season of *hope*. The air was cleared to some degree and a new commitment to mutual cooperation, sharing and support among the parties was felt. There seemed to be a growing feeling that internal battles would not help us win our external wars.

> **Suffering**
> **Perseverance**
> **Character**
> **Hope**

This particular learning experience was almost more than I could handle. However, I remember reading somewhere in that great text on leadership that we would never be given more than we could handle through God's grace.

Several years later, the physician who made the motion that night calling for the vote of no confidence asked for my forgiveness. I told him that I had forgiven him a long time ago. To be honest, he probably did me a favor and helped prolong my career by giving me a wake-up call.

"…we also rejoice in our sufferings, because we know that suffering produces perseverance; perseverance, character; and character, hope."
—Romans 5:3-4

INK BY THE BARREL

One of the greatest fears of a person who works in the public arena is to have your name "smeared" in a local newspaper or on a television news program. A good reputation is something that you work hard for all your life and you cherish it above most of your other possessions. One of my wars was conducted publicly, and to this day, I still do not know whether I won or lost.

Many of the hospitals in our state were founded and governed by public hospital authorities created by city or county governments, and our institution was one of these. Initially, these local governments financed, backed and/or subsidized the facilities and operations of the hospitals. In our case, over time, all such support had been discontinued, and we had even reimbursed the city which had provided bond support for the original hospital. We were now on our own to compete in the market with other private and corporate health systems, even though our mission still included the care of all who came to our door irrespective of their ability to pay.

Like many others, we had restructured our governing body into a private nonprofit board of directors to give us broader business expertise and diversity to help guide us. Interestingly, all the board members served without compensation and viewed this role as a community service. Though the hospital authority technically maintained ownership of the assets of the organization, the policy decisions and operational oversight became the responsibility of the new board.

State open record and open meeting (sunshine) laws had always applied to hospital authorities, and by policy, we had always conducted our operating board under the same provisions. Others, however, had taken a different position; they contended that a restructured organization was not subject to the open record/meeting laws.

The problem began when we started collaborating and consolidating some of our activities with other institutions in order to compete effectively from a business standpoint. In a particular joint venture which involved forming a new parent corporation, all the other parties except us had already taken the stance that open records/meetings did not apply in this instance. Therefore, this became our official policy.

Our local newspaper with which we had enjoyed good relations over the years challenged this position by filing suit in state court to make all our records and meetings in this venture open. From my point of view, this became doubly difficult because the newspaper's owner and publisher had been a friend of mine, our daughters were good friends in the same class, and we attended the same church. This was just the beginning of what would be a series of battles which lasted almost a year with our adversary having the resources of a daily newspaper. Unfortunately for me, the focus of the conflict including editorial attacks was directed at me personally.

(From My Perspective)

Living, working, playing and worshiping in a community which was being told that you are an evil person was not easy. In addition to covering the real issues involved in this dispute, the newspaper began requesting all sorts of information about me personally. My Form W-2's and expense reports for past years were examples. These were then in turn reported in various news articles in a manner which was highly distorted from my point of view. I was portrayed as being deceptive, dishonest and corrupt. I had been accustomed to being the "good guy" for many years in my community and now I was being regularly called the "bad guy" by my local newspaper. As in any war, there are bound to be casualties. The question was whether I would be among the dead or just the wounded.

(From the Other Side)

The news media has a responsibility to accurately provide information to the general public on issues affecting them. Information about their local hospital certainly falls into that category. Sunshine laws were designed to shed light on subjects of public interest and are specifically focused on government officials and agencies which serve the public. This assists in eliminating any abuse in authority and insures accountability. The issue of whether a private entity that is formed by a public authority is subject to the same legal provisions needs to be litigated and its legal status determined. If there is hesitancy or refusal to provide legitimately requested information, this implies that there is something to hide. Therefore, more and additional material will be sought under the law including the compensation of officials working in government-related institutions.

The problem with a public battle such as this is that it can be awfully one-sided. Our lawyer (who incidentally had been a legislator who helped write these sunshine laws and later became our governor) gave me some good advice. He said, "You don't need to be fighting publicly with an organization that buys ink by the barrel."

The initial ruling from the court was that under our particular structure, we were subject to the sunshine laws. Our board of directors chose not to appeal the ruling and let the decision stand. The newspaper won the legal battle. After that we returned to some degree of normalcy. To its credit, the newspaper was not unreasonable in its requests afterwards.

What did I learn from all this? I learned how to pray better and more often. But, I guess that the greatest lesson was to realize how important my reputation was to me.

> **The greatest lesson was to realize how important my reputation was to me.**

At that time I sang in our church choir and every Sunday from the choir loft I would see my former friend, the local newspaper publisher, ushering. Hate may be too strong and dislike may be too weak, but what ever the emotion was it blocked my ability to truly worship. I felt an intense need to seek reconciliation and forgiveness, not for fighting the war but for harboring bitterness. We met in his office early one morning and as a result I have forgiven and been forgiven, and I believe that a friendship has been restored. I don't honestly know whether he was right and I was wrong or whether I was right and he was wrong. Maybe we both were in some respects.

> *"He must also have a good reputation with outsiders, so that he will not fall into disgrace..."*
> —*1 Timothy 3:7*

THE RISE AND FALL OF AN EMPIRE

It is fascinating to look back and see where you have been because you are what you are today because you have been there. One of my favorite Broadway musicals is *Camelot*. It is about a fantasy kingdom headed by a wonderful king named Arthur. It was a place like no other where the good guys always won—a place where you just wanted to be. The words to the song, "Camelot," go like this, "In short there's simply not a more congenial spot for happ'ly ever-aftering than here in Camelot."[15] I don't know if everyone has a glimpse of a Camelot, but here is mine as I view it from a "yearning" perspective.

Before retirement, I served as CEO of *PROMINA Health System* located in Atlanta. *PROMINA* in a very short period grew to be one of the premier integrated health systems in the country. Now, just five years after my retirement, I am often asked by friends out of the area, "How is *PROMINA* doing?" I answer with a sense of regret and sadness, "It does not exist any more." Their response is usually, "Wow, how could that be?" Here is the story of *PROMINA*.

In the early 1990's, health care had become a market place commodity which was far different from my traditional view of it as a community service. Mergers and affiliations among providers (both hospitals and doctors) were the strategy for many. *Bigger* was equated with *better.* This was driven by the need to control costs, to be competitive and to gain a position of strength when negotiating with insurance and managed care companies. My organization, which at the time included two hospitals and a variety of ambulatory services, embraced the consolidation strategy.

Another community hospital in our immediate vicinity was likewise seeking comfort through the economies of scale. A joint laundry project between us had proven highly successful. Discussions were held at the highest level between our two organizations and, as a result, a full merger was accomplished. This was somewhat novel in our conservative community at the time, but our model generated the interest of others. We aspired to add more to our ranks. However, we discovered that a full merger of assets with other institutions in the area would be problematic. Political and governmental entities were involved with some, and each provided services to a unique section of the greater metropolitan area. An obvious tension existed between the need to be together in the marketplace and the desire to maintain autonomy in each community. As a result, a unique model was developed for our purposes. Without being too technical, I called it a *vitally* (similar but somewhat different from virtually) *integrated system*, which was to say it was to be a family of hospitals and doctors. It was vital that we worked together against what we viewed as a common enemy (market pressures).

The next two years brought four other local systems into the fold which collectively totaled 13 hospitals and over 2000 physicians.

The CEOs of all these joining institutions had been good friends and professional colleagues for many years. Some of the publicity which resulted in the formation of *PROMINA* implied that it was born out of the close relationships among its leaders. This mammoth effort was not without both internal and external challenges, but despite that we were launched and the empire was formed. Almost immediately, we became a force to be reckoned with in the market place. We purchased supplies, equipment and services together, standardized certain functions, marketed our services and most importantly negotiated insurance and managed care contracts together.

Our model gained popularity and recognition nationally. *PROMINA* was designated the number one integrated health system in the country. The American Hospital Association sponsored a national conference which we hosted in Atlanta touting our model. My picture appeared on the front of the cover of its journal. I was asked to speak at state, national and international conferences. Awards and honors kept coming to the organization and to me personally as its leader. What a ride it was professionally. I could not imagine a greater capstone on a career than going out as head of one of the great innovative organizations in my industry. Truly, it was Camelot!

BUT, just as the fable of Camelot did not end well, neither did the story of *PROMINA*. Sometimes there is one specific reason that an idea is lost or an enterprise fails. Viewing this retrospectively, I have concluded that there was one fundamental reason for *PROMINA's* failure. However, there were several components. For instance, health care had traditionally been viewed as a local community service and a cottage industry. Another level of organizational bureaucracy became burdensome. The attempt to marry hospitals and physicians conflicted with existing individual and group practice patterns.

Personalities and individual values clashed and eroded commitment among the institutional leaders. Unfortunately, even the questioning of personal integrity among some began to arise.

The lack of full integration of assets allowed a relative easy exit for the partners. A return to independence and autonomy appealed to some. Some of the competitive forces which brought the group together had subsided to some degree.

Some of the partners were stronger financially and felt that they were bringing more to the table than they were receiving. Shared power became an issue.

Cultural differences which did not seem so important at first became more significant as *PROMINA* evolved.

And, I'm sure there were other issues that I can not recall after several years.

All of the above ultimately clashed with the concept of an area-wide integrated health system. However, in the end all of these problems could have been overcome if there had been a universal belief that being a part of this system brought "value." The hard lesson that I gained from this is that no enterprise will survive and flourish in the long run unless it brings real as well as perceived value to those it serves. The fatal illness lasted about four years after the initial rupture in cohesiveness, and this organization which we once viewed as our salvation was laid to rest without fanfare or ceremony. I had already retired but as the initial leader of the pack, I could not help but feel a sense of abandonment, a bit of resentment, and personal sadness.

> **No enterprise will survive and flourish in the long run unless it brings real as well as perceived value to those it serves.**

I wish all stories could end with "happily ever after," but you know if that was the case this would not be earth but heaven.

"The ax is already at the root of trees, and every tree that does not produce good fruit will be cut down and thrown into the fire."
—Luke 3:9

A WAR WITHIN

Most of my war stories depict a conflict between me and an adversary. However, for leaders as well as followers, there are other types of wars—wars that may be fought within individuals themselves. These can be the most difficult because in some cases the battles may expose dark secrets and even character flaws. Let me share what I mean.

I grew up in the Deep South during the 1940-50's. I attended segregated schools, rode in the front of the city buses and worshiped in all-white churches. Despite this, I honestly don't remember believing that those of another skin color were inferior in any way. Rather, I thought it was the culture of the time that dictated a separation among the races. I do remember my dad, who was the pastor of a large church during those times, being asked, "What are we going to do if any black folks show up on Sunday morning for worship?" His answer, "They will worship!" was not popular with some of the parishioners.

I remember the trauma that accompanied the desegregation of public schools and the various events of the historic civil rights movement. Interestingly, the only African-American or even Asian students in any of my classes came during my final year in graduate school in Washington, D.C.

During my administrative residency, I was on night duty at the University of Alabama Hospital in Birmingham when the bombing of the black church that killed several children occurred. I witnessed the fire hoses being turned on those protesting in the streets. I was on administrative call at University Hospital during the race riot which occurred in 1970 in Augusta, Georgia. I have witnessed first hand the result of prejudice and discrimination, and even had friends who publicly condemned racism while practicing it privately in both word and deed.

I give you this background in order for you to understand the context for an important lesson that I wish to share. When I was appointed to my first chief executive position, the selection was made by the hospital's board of trustees. One of the board members was Mr. Charles Ferguson. Charlie, as we all called him, held a responsible position at Lockheed (one of the largest employers in our area) and was a very active community leader. He is also African-American and as a trustee was one of my bosses. This was my first experience working for a black man and to be perfectly honest, I probably subconsciously still carried some prejudicial baggage.

However, what a great experience that turned out to be! For the next 18 years, he was a mentor and advisor in areas to which no one else could relate. At almost every board meeting which was preceded by dinner, Mr. Ferguson would say our blessing. This in itself set the tone for objective, constructive and wise decision-making. Today, I love him as a friend and brother.

Some years later, Dr. James Fisher was nominated for board membership, and I was asked to meet and discuss the position with him. We needed some younger members, as well as an additional physician, on the board at the time. Jim, who was a highly respected internist, fit the bill perfectly.

I arrived at his office early before office hours to give us time to talk. While waiting, I noticed that there were several old western comic books on his desk. This was interesting to me because one of my favorite cowboys was Lash LaRue (who incidentally I had met personally). Therefore, we already had something in common. We immediately reminisced about going to the movie theaters in our small southern hometowns on Saturday for the western double features. Then Jim shared something that not only amazed me but also shook me to the core. He said, "You know, I had to sit up in the balcony when I was growing up with others like me, but I would look down at the folks below and realize that I had the best seat in the house." I truly wondered how a black man who had personally experienced such prejudice and discrimination would not be bitter and cynical. I went to win him over as a supporter, but I left that day with the highest respect for one who, too, would become one of my bosses. Today, I also consider him a friend and brother.

I will always be thankful for the relationships that I had with Mr. Charlie Ferguson and Dr. Jim Fisher. I was blessed and was a better leader because of their influence.

These and numerous other experiences have helped me win a battle within myself. This was not a conflict which I chose to have, but instead it was one that was somewhat inherent within me because of my cultural upbringing. I do not know whether I have fully won this particular battle, but with God's help I do believe that I have fought a good fight and kept the faith. We all have a war that we fight within ourselves. Whether we win or lose, these battles will determine the height of our values and the depth of our character.

> **We all have a war that we fight within ourselves. Whether we win or lose, these battles will determine the height of our values and the depth of our character.**

In this regard, I was encouraged one day when one of our African-American employees stopped by my office and asked me to go up to the nursery and see his new baby. As he walked out the door he said, "By the way, we have named our son Bernard after you and we are going to call him 'Bernie'."

"By this all men will know that you are my disciples,
if you love one another."
—John 13:35

WAR STORIES

"For though we live in the world, we do not wage war as the world does."
—*2 Corinthians 1:3*

Questions for Further Study and Discussion

Would you be willing to share a "War Story" that has occurred in your personal and/or professional life? If so, please cover the following:

1.   Give enough details (but not more than you feel comfortable divulging) so that others can understand the problems and issues. But be as brief and concise as possible.

2.   Define what you believe to be the one most important issue in the "war."

3.   Describe who you saw as the real enemy(s) and your current relationship with that person(s).

4.   If the battle was an internal one (fought within yourself), explain how you have attempted (or still attempting) to resolve it.

5.   Identify the winner(s) and loser(s).

6.   List the lessons learned from being a warrior in this encounter (no more than three).

7.   Describe what part your faith and beliefs played in this experience.

8.   Close by telling how this war story has affected you life.

A LESSON THAT SHOULD HAVE BEEN
LEARNED AT CHURCH

(The Church's Role in Christian Leadership Development)

"Be shepherds of the church of God..."
--Acts 20:28

Though this book addresses *leadership* in general, it has been particularly focused on *institutional leadership from a Christian perspective.* But there is something that should be learned in our churches about this subject. After all, the church is that earthly "institution" that God has ordained to communicate his message and carry out his mission.

Is the modern-day church fulfilling its obligation to those who desire to bridge the gap between their career paths and their faith journeys, particularly those in leadership positions? Is this great institution whose members are often leaders in their local communities helping them apply their faith in their jobs? Can we tell who are Christians and who are not as we interact with various organizations in our communities? One disillusioned young employee commented about her boss, "That same person that I worship with on Sunday is different from the one I work with during the week." Many of us (including myself) have routinely made our jobs and our faith "off limits" to each other.

The concept of bringing one's *career path* and one's *faith journey* together is a compelling one. In my early years, I am not certain that I even viewed it as an issue; however, there came a time when it became apparent to me that this is part of God's plan for us as individuals. It was then that my perspective on work, and even life in general, changed. It was clear that I needed to *bridge the gap.*

Having worked in healthcare, I always liked the analogy of the church as a "hospital for sinners." Among other things, it is a place where spiritual "diagnosis" and "treatment" should occur to assist us in our efforts toward an effective and productive Christian lifestyle. Spiritual well-being has many of the same requirements as physical/mental health. For example, the needs for proper nourishment, regular exercise and adequate rest are required in both realms. These all help prepare us for the "game of life" that is before us. Should not the church be our spiritual dining hall, gym and haven, the training ground for our most important game?

I am who I am because of many influencing factors, including my church community. However, though I have been an active member, most of my own leadership training came from sources other than my church. Our educational institutions from kindergarten to graduate school include the subject of leadership directly or indirectly in their curricula. Team sports, music and art groups, student government and even social clubs emphasize and promote leadership development. Most businesses, organizations and institutions throughout our society include programs to assist their current executives and prepare their future officers for leadership. My local community and state sponsors leadership programs—*Leadership Cobb* and *Leadership Georgia* to nurture the next generation of leaders.

Most of my leadership training came from sources other than my church.

Some may argue that enough leadership training programs already exist. But that is not what we are talking about here. We are talking about *Christian* leadership! Nearly 2,500 years ago, the ancient Chinese military philosopher Sun-Tzu said, "A poor leader, the people fear; a good leader, the people love; a great leader, the people say, 'We did it ourselves.'"[16] I would add, a Christian leader, the people say, "Introduced us to 'the' leader named Jesus!"

If leaders are to bridge the gap between their career paths and faith journeys, they must learn to lead like Jesus. There is a special role that our churches can play to help leaders in various institutional settings apply Christian principles in their jobs. And, in doing that, they would have a transforming, far-reaching influence on our society at large. Can you imagine what would happen if all Christians who occupy leadership roles actually put their faith into practice by turning their jobs into ministries! Truly, this would have a revolutionary effect.

What can or should our churches be doing in this regard? In attempting to answer this question, I draw upon my own personal experience immediately before, during and after the publication of the first edition of this book. As I accumulated and organized the material, I consulted with pastors, colleagues, friends and others who were in leadership positions. I had recently helped organize and initiate a Christian laity leadership program for the church denomination of which I am a member. I spoke about Christian leadership principles at church worship services, dinners, retreats and conferences; lectured at several universities; facilitated workshops for corporate leadership teams; delivered commencement addresses; and mentored/coached aspiring executives. Without exception, in all these venues, which include religious, governmental and private institutional settings, these activities were met with enthusiasm and an eagerness to learn more. I attribute this not to my own abilities, but to an innate desire among many to get their professional and spiritual lives in sync.

The message is clear. Christian leadership principles should be regularly fostered and taught in our churches. But, on closer inspection, I found little evidence of it being done. In fact, a cursory survey of

Christian seminaries revealed that very little practical leadership training is offered for future pastors (Chief Spiritual Officers).

It's high time the church got into the business of Christian leadership development! (So, here is my proposal.)

START WITH THE CHURCH'S OWN LEADERSHIP TEAM

Since my retirement I have worked part-time in education and consulting positions. (Consulting engagements are often needed when organizations are experiencing problems or going in the wrong direction.) The idea is to have a qualified and objective view from an outside source to assist in solving problems and reversing negative trends. So in regard to the church's championing Christian leadership development, I am engaging myself as a consultant for this task.

Most main-line churches in our country have seen a decline in membership and attendance. The average age of pastors and members in my own denomination is 58 and 60, respectively. Often, less than a third of the church membership can be classified as active (attending and financially supporting regularly). Some have even made the observation that our society's past couple of generations have created a new type of religious practice – "*Casual* Christianity." Casual in this context does not refer to the dress code for church but instead to the seriousness of one's approach to the Christian faith. Unfortunately, such a practice naturally leads to spiritual impotence - not only with individuals but also within the churches.

> **Casual Christianity... leads to spiritual impotence – not only with individuals but also within the churches.**

Certainly, there are many problems and issues that contribute to the current condition of these traditionally strong religious institutions. However, I am of the opinion that *lack of leadership* is one of the major contributing factors. I have heard horror stories of new pastors being "thrown to the wolves" as they enter their initial pastorates lacking the skills and knowledge needed to lead their congregations. And likewise, many committed laity in churches become disillusioned and frustrated with their pastors' inability to provide effective leadership. I can recall in my own experience as a healthcare executive the problems facing many professionally-trained individuals who were promoted into supervisory and management positions. Had we not offered additional and continual training and support, their new leadership roles would have been very difficult to fill despite the fact that they were previously excellent performers in their fields of expertise.

I would be first to acknowledge that these problems do not rest exclusively with new clergy. As in other professions, some sincerely committed pastors have floundered because of their lack of leadership abilities. Others have moved from highly effective to virtually unproductive status for various reasons such as burnout, personal problems, "end of career" syndrome, and others.

Based on these observations I recommend to the clergy in our churches that:

• The curriculum in seminaries include in-depth courses in Christian leadership principles taught by experienced, seasoned leaders.

• Continuing Education (CE) programs focusing on leadership be developed and required on a periodic basis for active clergy (similar to CE credits for other professionals).

• Clergy include "Christian leadership" in their preaching and teaching topics and in related support programs, thereby emphasizing the subject with their congregations.

- Senior clergy assist in the continual development of junior clergy and other staff members for leadership positions that they currently or will occupy.

- The clergy equip themselves to serve as catalysts for laity leadership development within their congregations.

What about Christian leadership development for the church's laity? An evolving concept that many successful churches are embracing is the pastor's role in equipping and empowering the laity for ministry.

Several years ago, I was asked to organize a new program to prepare laity for church leadership positions at the local, district and conference levels. It evolved into a year-long program which included four weekend workshops. Formal presentations by various speakers and facilitators assisted the participants in discovering and understanding their churches, their spiritual gifts, their shared ministry and their leadership skills. Additionally, small groups were established within each class to study and analyze church and societal issues/problems and to offer recommendations/solutions. Over two hundred have already graduated from LEADERSHIP UMC* and this program has become a model for Christian laity training in our denomination. I share this with you because it is an example of what I believe should be offered and implemented in one form or another in all churches. In large churches it could be customized; in small churches it could be a shared program. Drawing on my experience with this particular project and as part of my consulting engagement, I would recommend that:

- Church laity be encouraged and required in certain cases (those holding top leadership positions) to participate in Christian leadership training offered either internally and/or as part of a shared program.

- Clergy, along with laity in all churches, devote a significant amount of time to improving communication and program effectiveness through a commitment to *shared ministry.* And, in so doing they should work toward creating an environment of cooperation, respect and service.

*Example of responses from participants in <u>LEADERSHIP UMC:</u>

"I have never participated in a program that returns so much to each participant…"

"LEADERSHIP UMC has helped me to take my lay ministry to another level…"

"In my thirty years of senior management I have not attended a better program on basic leadership principles…"

"…appointed elders for them in each church and, with prayer and fasting, committed them to the Lord, in whom they had put their trust."
--Acts 14:23

CHRISTIAN LEADERSHIP OUTSIDE THE WALLS OF THE CHURCH

The dynamics between clergy and laity within a church are interesting and the potential impact when they work together as a team is phenomenal. Let me use my own church as an example. One of the larger congregations in our area, it has three fulltime ordained pastors and approximately 3800 members. This means that for each pastor there are over 1200 lay persons. When asked how many ministers we have I usually say, "3" but shouldn't I be answering, "3803!" That is the potential if we do this right.

The question then becomes, "How do we (the church) motivate, equip and empower our members to be leaders in ministry in their own individual spheres of influence outside the walls of the church?" One of the most effective ways to accomplish this is to teach church members how to use Christian leadership principles regardless of the setting. In my own experience, I have seen an amazing multiplying effect when just one individual leads like Jesus! You don't have to *explain* it. You just have to *do* it. Servant leadership can be a powerful instrument in the Christian's tool box. And our text book, the Holy Bible, contains all the instructions we will need.

> **I have seen an amazing multiplying effect when just one individual leads like Jesus!**

In this area, I recommend that:

• The church become a hub for group and individual Christian leadership development for application in outside secular settings;
• Church libraries include material on this important subject;
• Courses be offered to church members and the community using internal expertise or external resources such as books like this or other available references, tapes, videos, etc.
• Existing groups within the church be encouraged to include programs on Christian leadership development principles among their scheduled events;
• The Church facilitate coaching/mentoring programs for emerging leaders;
• The Church research and identify "best practices" in other churches and share knowledge;
• Each church become a "Learning Organization."

When we think of "institutional leadership," major corporations, businesses, churches, schools, governments and the like usually come to mind. However, one of the greatest institutions in our society and perhaps the most significant is the family. Despite its importance, about one-half of all marriages end in divorce; child abuse is at epidemic levels; and in some communities more babies are born out of wedlock than in established families. And of those families that continue to exist as a unit, many are dysfunctional! Hundreds of books have been written and thousand of remedies have been suggested to address problems on marriage and family. I would add my two cents worth to this discussion. I honestly believe that Christian leadership principles need to be practiced in this most vital institution in our society – *the family*. If heads of our homes would learn to lead like Jesus, many of our families' problems would be solved. A great opportunity exists for providing resources and training in Christian *family* leadership.

∾

After the initial edition was published, I was asked by a book distributor if I was passionate about my book. He felt this was imperative for its success. I thought for a minute and said, "No, but I am passionate about the message in it." I would now add that I am even more passionate about the message contained in this addition to this work. *Our churches need to be a primary source for Christian leadership development and training.* Certainly, the church's primary role is worship, evangelism, missions, and the like, but all these areas require effective *leaders* to guide the process - particularly outside the church's walls. If leadership development became a focus, we would no longer hear anyone say, "This is **a lesson that 'should' have been learned at church.**"

"Be strong and courageous, because you will lead the people…"
--Joshua 1:6

A LESSON THAT SHOULD HAVE BEEN LEARNED AT CHURCH

"Be shepherds of the church of God..."
—Acts 20:28

Questions for Further Study and Discussion

1. Did you receive any leadership training at your church? If so, in what form?

2. Is your church growing or declining in active membership and support? To what do you attribute this?

3. Are very many community leaders active in your church?

4. In your mind is there a difference between leadership and Christian leadership? What is it?

5. Do you know leaders who act differently on Sunday than the rest of the week?

6. Is the development of Christian leaders a part of your church's mission? If so, is it for inside leadership or beyond the church's walls?

7. Does family leadership from a Christian perspective receive any focus in your church?

8. Should Christian leadership development become a part of your church's program? If so, how would you approach it? Is your pastor assisting in equipping and empowering you for ministry? How?

9. Is there a gap between your own career path and faith journey? Do you want to bridge the gap? How are you going to do it?

REFLECTIONS AND CONCLUSIONS

"And we, with unveiled faces all reflect the Lord's glory..."
—*2 Corinthians 3:18*

My dad was a preacher, and I, like most boys, gave some thought to doing what he did when I grew up. In my generation, some even thought that a son was a bit disloyal if he didn't follow in his father's footsteps. I always felt a tug in that direction until another preacher who was a close friend of my dad's told me that our society needed more Christians in the business world than in the pulpit. Since my gifts and passions were in that direction, I took that encouragement from Pastor Joe to be God's way of pointing me toward my life's work.

However, after I arrived at my professional pinnacle, I felt an emptiness and lack of fulfillment that should not accompany such achievement. What do you do if your *life's work* and your *faith journey* seem to be out of sync, particularly if you are in a leadership role? I began to wonder if I had answered the wrong call. Then another pastor and dear friend, in one of his best sermons, gave me help and clarity. Pastor Charles said, "Your calling may not be to do something different but instead it may be to do what you are doing differently." That intensified my quest to learn how to do my job *differently* by seeking guidance from the One who has the answers.

> **Your calling may not be to do something different
> but instead it may be to do what you are doing
> differently.**

I needed to write this final chapter to let those of you who have so graciously read my stories, know exactly where I'm coming from.

To share one's faith in something is not always easy. It carries risks, for it can be misinterpreted, misunderstood, or outright rejected. However, to fail to at least make the attempt carries even greater consequences. Someone may miss a very significant message that could positively influence his or her life, or even save it. Therefore, I offer these few reflections on my faith in God, upon which these writings were based.

"Reflections" is a good word. I believe the job of every Christian is to reflect Jesus Christ to the world. We are like mirrors that can give back or exhibit the image that they receive. In this world, we may be the only Jesus some will ever see. That is why it is extremely vital to be cleansed and purified so that the reflection will be clear and recognizable to others. I hope these final few thoughts and beliefs (reflections) will be helpful to you.

SPIRITUAL CHANGE

Sometimes I wish that I had a dramatic personal testimony to share that had a highly contrasting before and after – an autobiography that was a tale of spiritual *"rags to riches."* But fortunately, I guess, my life has not been filled with those kinds of traumatic experiences.

To further indicate what I mean, let me share this illustration with you. In early America, an Indian brave would select his pony by one of two means. He could go up into the hills, capture a wild pony and then "break" him. Or he could gradually cultivate the trust of a pony that grazed near the village, and then one day just mount it, encountering little or no resistance from the animal. I'm like the second pony. I have known the Lord as far back as I can remember; I grazed in the churchyard all my life. However, there is no doubt my love and trust have continued to grow over the years because of his grace and mercy. My point is that we all need some type of a spiritual change, whether it is instantaneous or gradual, from being lost to being found.

> **We all need some type of a spiritual change, whether it is instantaneous or gradual, from being lost to being found.**

"...he was lost and is found."
—Luke 15:24

A GREAT SIN

Like all human beings, my greatest weakness has been my sinful nature, which separates me from God. Though I did not have to be saved from sins such as murder, drunkenness, drug addiction, adultery (those we often call the big sins), I had to admit to and ask forgiveness for one sin (among many others) that I have come to believe may be the most serious of them all. I had constantly been committing the sin of *lukewarmness*. God said, *"I know your deeds, that you are neither cold nor hot...so because you are lukewarm, I am about to spit you out of my mouth"* (Revelation 3:15-16). I don't know about you, but I like food either hot or cold. Lukewarm food is not only less tasteful but spoils much more easily. Similarly, God has said that he doesn't want lukewarm followers; they make him nauseous. I don't think this means we need to be constantly preaching at others, but it does mean continually serving them like Jesus did. Our apathy and timidity in appropriately practicing and sharing our faith, particularly in our work, are manifestations of our lukewarm tendencies. I mention this specifically because many other Christians have shared with me their own guilt of this sin I call *lukewarmness*.

> Our apathy and timidity in appropriately
> practicing and sharing our faith, particularly in our
> work, are manifestations of our
> lukewarm tendencies.

"...because you are lukewarm...I am about to
spit you out of my mouth."
—Revelation 3:16

A NOUN

From a grammatical standpoint, I have been intrigued by the word *Christian*. The dictionary includes it as both a noun and an adjective, and we often use it in both contexts. **A noun is the name of something whereas an adjective is the modifier of a noun (a descriptive term).** But somehow, "*Christian*" seems to me to be more appropriate as a noun.

Once, prior to delivering a speech, I was introduced as a Christian (adjective) CEO. I felt honored to have Christ's name attached to my position. However, someday I hope I will be called a Christian (noun) who was incidentally a chief executive officer. Certainly, it is my desire to *act* like a Christian, but more importantly, I want to *be* one. This may be just a play on words to you, but the distinction is an important one to me.

> **It is my desire to *act* like a Christian, but more**
> **importantly, I want to *be* one.**

"The disciples were called Christians first at Antioch."
—Acts 11:26

SAVIOR AND LORD

In order to experience the full benefits of being a Christian, I have learned that we must not only accept Jesus Christ as our personal *Savior*, but we also need to make him the *Lord* of our lives. By this, I mean turning over all aspects of our lives to him. I have concluded that most people in our society believe in God; many accept Jesus as their Savior; some even turn over portions of their lives to him, but few give all areas of their lives to the Lord. When I prayed for his lordship over all of my life, including my job, it was then that my real spiritual journey began in earnest.

It is a matter of yielding ourselves to him. In truth, *in order to yield (produce) fruit, we must first yield (surrender) our will.* Remember that when the traditional triangular organization chart is flipped upside down it takes the form of a highway *yield* sign.

Additionally, to be able to ask and have someone else help carry life's load is in itself a God-send. One of my favorite nurses, with whom I had the pleasure of working for many years, gave me a plaque that sat on the top of my desk. It said, "Lord, help me to remember that nothing is going to happen today that you and I can't handle. Amen."

> **In order to yield (produce) fruit, we must first yield (surrender) our will.**

*"But grow in the grace and knowledge of our
Lord and Savior Jesus Christ."*
—*Peter 3:18*

THE CHOICE

In conclusion, I would offer just one last thought. We all have conscious choices to make in this life. I made mine to follow Jesus. I don't do it very well at times, but I'm committed to finishing the race by following that course. The greatest book ever written, the *Holy Bible*, is our instruction manual; we need to study it more. The greatest man who ever lived, *Jesus Christ*, the Son of God, is our role model; we need to emulate him more. God is our *Heavenly Father*; we need to talk with him more. The *Holy Spirit* is our guide and counselor; we need to listen more. I believe it is our responsibility to share, serve and care during our presence here on earth.

I hope and pray that some of these reflections and stories were meaningful to you. And that you, too will learn the lessons I learned on the way down.

> **We all have conscious choices to make in this life.
> I have made mine to follow Jesus.**

"But as for me and my household, we will serve the Lord."
—Joshua 24:15

God loves you and I do, too!

—Bernie Brown

REFLECTIONS AND CONCLUSIONS

"And we, with unveiled faces all reflect the Lord's glory..."
—*2 Corinthians 3:18*

Questions for Personal Introspection

1. In your work, should you be doing something different or should you be doing what you do, differently?

2. Are you reflecting Jesus Christ to the world through your life and work? Is the reflection clear and recognizable?

3. Does your testimony reflect an instantaneous or gradual conversion?

4. Are you a lukewarm Christian? If so, what do you need to do to change?

5. Are you an "adjective" or "noun" Christian?

6. Do you believe in God? Have you accepted Jesus Christ as your personal savior? Is he lord of some parts of your life? Are you willing to make him lord of all your life including your work?

EPILOGUE

THE LAST LESSON

This book is all about lessons and leadership. But perhaps the most important lesson is being added after everything else has been completed. The manuscript was already being edited and I was waiting to review any changes suggested by the professionals. Snookie and I planned to spend several days with Amanda, our youngest daughter and her three children while her husband Brad was on a mission trip to Uruguay. (This was part of his training for ministry at Southern Seminary in Louisville, Ky.)

Nathan, their middle child and our youngest grandson, had experienced an elevated fever off and on for several weeks and his doctors were attempting to determine the cause. We had planned to attend Easter Sunday services at their church, but it was obvious that little Nathan, who is three years old, was not feeling well enough to go. So, I volunteered to stay home with him. As I watched a church service on television, Nathan became more and more uncomfortable, so I held and rocked him until everyone returned. Amanda had called the doctor earlier and an appointment was already scheduled for Monday morning.

The doctor's visit included more tests and analyses because of the persistent fever and discomfort. When they arrived home afterwards, Amanda was apprehensive but positive; the doctor was to call with test results and further treatment plans that afternoon. None of us realized the doctor's call would change our lives forever.

Our immediate and extended family circle had experienced the normal ups and downs of life—people getting married, having babies, growing through pains and challenges, getting sick and then getting well, experiencing good and bad jobs, moving and changing, living long and dying well, etc. We had often wondered why we had been so blessed in this regard while observing others suffer so much in many different ways.

The phone rang and Amanda went into the bedroom to talk with the doctor. When she came out, tears flowed down her cheeks as she shared that the test results were pointing toward possible leukemia and that an appointment was set for the next day with a pediatric oncologist.

Daddies and granddaddies are supposed to be strong, but Amanda and her dad wept together for a long time. Nathan and I, whom he calls "Pappy," have a special relationship.

The next few days were filled with continuous activity. Brad had been kept informed and was attempting to get a flight home immediately. Nathan was admitted to the Children's Hospital. Additional lab tests, bone marrow analyses, x-rays, CT scans, and MRIs followed. Leukemia was ruled out but a tumor was discovered on my grandson's kidney. (Of course, Amanda's immediately reaction was "Nathan can have one of mine!") The initial findings (which would be confirmed later) indicated the growth was malignant and had spread.

Nathan's older brother Jordan and I picked up Brad at the airport He and Amanda spent the next two weeks between home and the hospital, learning and planning for that which would follow. Chemotherapy, a bone marrow transplant, surgery, monitoring—many life-style changes were all in the picture.

During the early days of this discovery, we cried privately and together. We hugged a lot and tried to keep everyone in our circles informed. We all came to realize that only God knows the future, but we are so thankful that we *know* God.

What is the lesson in all this? There are hundreds probably, but the one I have gained is this. *ANYONE CAN LEAD!*

Certainly little Nathan did not choose this fate nor would we have chosen it for him. However, mountains are being moved by him. The serious illness of a child touches everyone, and this little fellow is already having an impact on many, many lives. The faith of his mom and dad are stronger than ever and they are ministering to others even as they meet the challenges each day brings.

Jordan's love of his little brother Nathan demonstrates God's love in its simplest and most powerful form. (Jordan is only five years old but his prayers for his brother are delivered straight to the gates of heaven.) Greta, their little sister, raises the spirits of all with the joy exhibited by a typical one year old. Family members are being drawn closer together, many reevaluating their priorities. Old as well as new friends are focused on caring and praying. Churches are experiencing revival as they pray for healing. One pastor said, "The Holy Spirit was present, and felt by our congregation when Nathan's situation was announced." The internet is alive with messages of hope from all over the world through *CaringBridge*. The telephone has become an instrument of goodwill. During the first days in the hospital, a *PrayerPager* vibrated (and entertained Nathan) with every prayer dialed in at a rate of one every thirty seconds. And the mailboxes were filled with much more than bills and advertisements.

All Christians by nature have an innate desire to introduce others to the Lord. This has been my desire since I met him many years ago. However, I truly believe that little Nathan (who incidentally is named for the Old Testament prophet) has had more influence in this regard in just two weeks than I have had in a lifetime.

Again, the lesson here is that leadership comes in all sizes and forms. However, the important thing is probably not *who* or *how* but instead, *where* one leads others. Nathan has led me and possibly several thousand others to a closer and stronger relationship with Jesus.

When he is healed, our heavy hearts will be lightened. In the meantime, I will continue to praise God from whom all blessings flow.

> **The important thing is probably not *who* or *how* but instead, *where* one leads others.**

"...and a little child will lead them."
—Isaiah 11:6

WHY? Reflections of Grandparents
(One year later)

As grandparents we find ourselves in a uniquely vulnerable position when our grandchildren are involved. Our joy is doubled when our grandchildren make us proud by the way they act or how they succeed in their endeavors. From the moment they are born through potty training, walking, talking…starting school, participating in sports and the arts, excelling in academics, graduating…working, marrying, etc.; we grandparents glory in it all. The reason for our "double" joy is that these children belong to our children! We get to treasure these experiences on two levels because of the love we have for them both!

Unfortunately, the reverse is also true. When our grandchildren experience pain or adversity of any kind, our own suffering is magnified. By giving us the capacity to care so deeply, God also allows us the possibility of hurting profoundly. This is because we recognize the heartache being felt by our children and we long to be able to "fix it" for them as we did when they were young. Most of us don't normally dwell on thoughts like this. At least we didn't until our precious grandson, Nathan became ill.

Nathan's primary diagnosis made in April of 2007 was neuroblastoma (stage IV), a relatively rare form of cancer affecting only about six hundred children nationwide each year. As we observed the influence of this disease on his little body and his heroic battle against it, we experienced the ramifications of this roller coaster ride on our family and on many others supporting us along the way.

When we first learned of Nathan's serious condition, we individually and then collectively confessed our initial reaction. It was "WHY US, LORD!" Nothing like this had ever happened before in our immediate or extended families. The whole thing seemed so unfair! Nathan's dad, Brad McLean, was completing seminary and preparing to do God's work fulltime. Having willingly given up a successful engineering career, he and our daughter, Amanda, were already making plans to serve a church in a small community. Nothing about this turn of events made sense!

Of course, when we look back on our own upbringing, we remember being told, "Life is not always fair!" We even said it to our own children. However, until Nathan became ill we probably didn't really believe it. Throughout this entire experience, we have read the Bible much more often, but we still haven't found in those Holy Scriptures that life is supposed to be fair! To the contrary, there are many examples of unfairness. Yet, we are discovering that life can be victorious, abundant and eternal regardless of the circumstances.

Bad things are going to happen to good people and good things are going to happen to bad people. Life can throw things at us that can send us spinning out of control! The issue then becomes not *what* might happen, but more importantly, *how* we, with God's help, deal with what comes our way.

In addition to our personal feelings, numerous reactions and observations have come from many sources. For example, it was interesting to hear the responses of *our* parents (Nathan's great-grandparents) as we related our deep anguish concerning our little grandson. When we confessed the "double emotional whammy" that we were feeling, they in turn reported the "triple whammy" for them! They have love and concern filtering down through us to their grandchildren and on to the great-grandchildren. This reinforced a new understanding of the great breadth and depth of love that God gives to families!

Brad and Amanda have regularly communicated with thousands locally and around the world following their story. In fact, this has become a very real part of their own personal ministry. Between ten and fifteen thousand visits per month have been made to Nathan's internet website on *CaringBridge,* many of those signing the guestbook with notes of encouragement, expressions of newfound faith, and love letters to a little boy. Certainly, this has been a physical battle on the part of a gallant young warrior and his family. But not only that, it has been an amazing spiritual journey for many, many folks including these two grandparents.

As we experienced the emotions of fear, despair, hurt, concern, faith, hope, joy and love, our question changed. Instead of defiantly shouting, "WHY US, LORD!" we came to meekly ask, "Why *Not* Us,

Lord?" Many have walked this path before us. Many others are walking it now. Why *not* us! And, beyond that, why not allow us the privilege of sharing God's mercy and grace through it all!

We hope and pray that these reflections presented through the eyes of two very typical grandparents will be helpful to you during your journey through life. As we perform our various roles on life's stage, may our tragedies be turned into victories. Jesus set the example!

Why Not Us, Lord!

—Snookie and Bernie Brown

From the journal of Brad and Amanda McLean, Nathan's parents (one year after his diagnosis)

During this year since Nathan's initial diagnosis he has spent 24 weeks in the hospital; made more than 50 additional clinic and outpatient visits; been eye-balled by doctors over 350 times; received 100 blood and platelet transfusions; been given regiments from 30 different anti-bacterial, anti-fungal, anti-viral and other helper drugs; had two stem cell transplants; received numerous rounds of chemotherapy and an unknown total level of exposure to radiation; had multiple surgical procedures including the removal of a malignant tumor and gone 50 days without nourishment by mouth. During this time, 150 meals have been provided by the family's church; Nathan was prayed over more than 75 times at the hospital; cards and letters fill up a very large box at home; more than 5,000 messages of love, encouragement, thoughts and prayers have been transmitted on Nathan's CaringBridge link with over 160,000 individual visits made to it; grandparents spent 24 weeks in Kentucky helping when Nathan was in the hospital or under intensive treatment; and other help and financial support are beyond calculation.

In April 2008, Brad was called to be pastor of the Lake Dreamland Baptist Church in Louisville, KY located less than 30 minutes from home.

Nathan remains under the excellent care and treatment of the doctors and staff at the Kosair Children's Hospital. On the first anniversary of this journey the report was as follows: "As of today, as precarious as 'today' is for all of us, Nathan stands in remission and the rest of the family stands with him!"

Update – 2012

Nathan has been in remission for five years. He has some physical limitations as a result of a brain infection that occurred during a second stem cell transplant. He is now in the second grade in the Cobb County (GA) public school system where his family has relocated. He just earned his second level karate belt where his instructor, during the award ceremony, stated, "Though Nathan has more reasons than any other to say, 'I can't,' he always says, 'I can!'" Jordan is in middle school and Greta is a first-grader. Dad, Brad, is a bi-vocational pastor at Pebblebrook Baptist Church and financial officer/pastor with Blue Skies Ministries. Mom, Amanda, is a substitute teacher and choir accompanist.

NOTES

Scripture passages taken from *The Holy Bible*, New International Version (NIV), Copyright 1973, 1978, 1986, 1986 by Zondervan Bible Publishers unless otherwise noted. All rights reserved.

End Notes

1. L. Peter and R. Hull, *The Peter Principle*, (New York, NY: William Morrow & Company, Inc.), 1969.
2. V. Lombardi, *Run to Daylight* (Englewood Cliffs, NJ: Prentice-Hall, 1984), p. 24.
3. A. Alda, from an address at Columbia University, 1979.
4. J. Nesbit, *Megatrends*, (New York, NY: Warner Books, 1982), p. 19.
5. Excerpts from a collection of "thoughts for the day" maintained by this writer. The original author is unknown.
6. M. Gandhi, from a collection of "thoughts for the day" maintained by this writer.
7. W. Rogers, collection.
8. D. Seaburg, collection.
9. G. Poulard, collection
10. O. W. Holmes, collection.
11. J. F. Dulles, collection.
12. W. A. Ward, collection.
13. Letter reprinted with the permission of William K. Leydecker and William J. Leydecker.
14. L. Kaiser, from a presentation, date and location unknown.
15. A.J. Lerner and F. Loewe, (London: Chappell & Co.), 1961.
16. Sun-Tzu, collection.

Bernie Brown is also the author of

PURPOSE IN THE FOURTH QUARTER
Finishing the Game of Life Victoriously

Visit www.purposeinthefourthquarter.com

Author's E-mail address:
bernielb@bellsouth.net

CPSIA information can be obtained at www.ICGtesting.com
Printed in the USA
LVOW080544060313

322849LV00001B/3/P